DAIWI

DEDICATION

This book is dedicated to the Nungs, who valiantly served under my command, all the other brave soldiers who fought alongside me, and to my wife, Lisa, to whom I owe heartfelt appreciation for her love and support.

CONTENTS

D A I W I

**A Personal And Poignant Account of
A MACV/SOG Special Forces Hero**

**"Silver wings upon their chest
These are men, America's best
One hundred men we'll test today
But only three win the Green Beret"**

"Ballad Of The Green Berets"
Written by SSgt. Barry Sadler and Robin Moore
1966

INTRODUCTION

Hanoi 1993. The best and the brightest were in Vietnam again, and so was I. Twenty-five years earlier, in some ways, this phrase described me. In 1968, I may not have been the best or the brightest, but I was certain I stood next to them. Not because I was a Special Forces Captain, a West Point graduate, football player, Ivy League dropout, or that I came from a Park Avenue penthouse. It was because in Vietnam I was free. In 1968, virtually without constraint, I roamed the jungles, cities, and mountain towns of Vietnam and Laos for nine months. I picked up scraps of newspaper in Da Nang whorehouses or the Saigon Bachelor Officer Quarters and read about the Summer of Love in the USA, about this or that—live and laugh. I spent years earning the right to be there: Airborne, Ranger, and Pathfinder schools, at Fort Benning, and with the U. S. 10th Special Forces in Bad Tolz, Germany. I trained alongside the British Special Air Service (SAS), French Marine Commandos (the equivalent of U. S. Navy SEALS), Deutsch Kampfschwimmers (German Special Forces), Special Forces Legionnaires (French Foreign Legion), Danish Jaeger Forces (Elite Special Forces Unit of the Royal Danish Army), and the Hellenic Raiders (Elite Greek 1st Raider/Paratrooper Brigade). These were the killer elite of every western war from Hitler on. For me, freedom came down to one word: meritocracy. It made every human construct from politics and economics to ethics and metaphysics seem pale and powerless.

Only a few top military or government officials had heard of a top-secret group that became an important part of my life when I graduated West Point's "Long Gray Line" in 1965. In 1964, the Joint Chiefs of Staff created an organization named SOG, as a subsidiary to the Military Assistance Command. An unconventional warfare task force, this group would be used in top-secret and cross-border reconnaissance operations in Cambodia and Laos in the Vietnam War. SOG consisted of soldiers from all branches of the military, including recon men and special operations pilots of the 90th Special Operations Wing, but predominately Army Special Forces. However, in March 1965, just a month or so before my graduation, SOG's Saigon headquarters very quietly celebrated finally being allowed to penetrate the Ho Chi Minh Trail, a highly strategic and important move. I had no way to know I would become a part of the secret forages and battles in forbidden Laos under the SOG banner. Had I known, my core would have recoiled in protest and fear, but I would have gone and done what I could for my country. General George C. Marshall, Chief of Staff, U.S. Army, World War II: "I want an officer for a secret and dangerous mission. I want a West Point Football Player." I was.

On March 8, 1965, the very first American combat troops from the 3/9 Marine Battalion came ashore on the beaches just Northwest of Da Nang. The event was televised and met with a boisterous show of support from sightseers. South Vietnamese officers, Vietnam girls with leis and four American soldiers with signs reading, "Welcome Gallant Marines." General Westmoreland, Senior U.S. Military Commander in Saigon, was appalled. He had hoped to keep the landing as quiet as possible.   When I finally arrived in Saigon and went to war, the campaign that America called the TET offensive was winding down. Vietnam called it The War Against Americans To Save the Nation, or the American War. The Communist TET offensive was two-fold: Create unrest in South Vietnam's populace and cause the U. S to scale back its support of the Saigon regime, or complete U. S. withdrawal. In an attack planned by General Vo Nguyen Giap, over 100 cities in South Vietnam were attacked by over 70,000 Communist troops. General Giap was thought by many to be one of the greatest politicians and military strategists of the 20th Century. Militarily, TET was a failure for the North Vietnamese Army and the rebel Viet Cong, but it was a strategic victory. American media wrongly portrayed the TET offensive as a Communist victory. Liberal propaganda was instrumental in turning the American populace against this long and bloody War. TET was not just about winning short-term battles. It proved to be an American political turning point in the war, leading to the slow withdrawal of United States troops from the region. Warfare had gone from permanent (Uncle Ho's) to ugly (ours) to unconditional. There is simply no greater meritocracy. I was headed to the very unconditional I

Corps, a member of SOG: the Project. SOG was a typically polite acronym (Studies and Observation Group) for a network of reconnaissance, saboteurs and assassins led by Colonel (later Major General) John Singlaub. The Joint Chiefs of Staff implemented the Project in 1964, as a subsidiary of the Military Assistance Command (MACV), during the secret war against Laos. The enemy terrain, and the obscure nature of civil war made it clear we badly needed covert activity. SOG had since become one of the backbones of the official war as well (it was a SOG operation, for example, that precipitated the Gulf of Tonkin), with Vietnam as our official mandate. To bastardize Melville, my "Yale and Harvard" was always Laos.

The Americans named the Ho Chi Minh Trail after the North Vietnamese President. The Communists called it the Truong Son after the Annamite Mountain Range in central Vietnam that runs from North Vietnam to South Vietnam, through Laos and Cambodia. The Trail was strategic for enemy communications and the transport of supplies during all wars in Vietnam. Part of what became the Trail had existed for centuries as primitive footpaths to facilitate trade in the region. The U. S. National Security Agency's official history of the Vietnam War stated that the Ho Chi Minh Trail was one of the greatest achievements in military engineering. Vietnam was divided into four corps of tactical political and military jurisdictions. I Corps, in the northernmost region of the country, covered 10,000 square miles and abutted Laos on the west and enemy bases supplied via the Ho Chi Minh Trail. The number of North Vietnam troops was estimated around 78,000 in I Corps, with about half of them around the DMZ. The next largest number was massed around Da Nang and could attack from either direction and could shell northern Quang Tri from North Vietnam and Laos. I Corps bordered the DMZ as well. Of the four tactical zones, I Corp, because of its location, was most likely to be attacked and hardest to protect or defend. I was assigned to I Corps, close to Marble Mountain that has approximately 156 steps to the top. I commanded soldiers up those steps many times. The terrain around I Corps favored the enemy. Rolling piedmont gave way to flat wetlands, mostly covered with rice paddies. Beyond that, the sand of the South China Sea stretched long and hot. Most of the Vietnamese inhabitants in the I Corps area lived in hamlets and villages interspersed around the rice fields, or in the large cities of Hue and Da Nang. The enemy's political agents and guerilla fighters lived and operated among the citizens and could easily obtain recruits and supplies. They still lived there, but I am certain it became much harder for them to obtain supplies after we showed up to interdict their operations. Much, much, harder. II Corps was the Central Highlands, III was a densely populated region between Saigon and the Highlands, and IV was the marsh Mekong Delta, in the southernmost region.

As a direct result of the Geneva Conference, in a peace-making effort between North and South Vietnam, the DMZ (demilitarized zone) in Vietnam was established and finalized in July 1954, at the end of the 8-year First Indochina War. The combat-free zone, also known as the 17th parallel, was a five-kilometer, or a little over three-mile area, and ran east and west, separating North and South Vietnam. During the Second Indochina war (Vietnam War), North Vietnam became known as the Democratic Republic of Vietnam. It was controlled almost entirely by the Communist Viet Minh, under the leadership of Ho Chi Minh. The south part of Vietnam became known as the independent State of Vietnam, first under the leadership of Bao Dai beginning in 1926. The State of Vietnam later became the Republic of Vietnam. As one can see, Vietnam was, and undoubtedly still is, a study in complicated politics.

During the 1940s and 1950s the United States and Britain collaborated on the development of herbicides for possible use in war. The British were the first to use these herbicides when the Malayan Communist Party attempted an overthrow of the British colonial administration. This resulted in a 12-year war from 1948-1960, named the Malayan Emergency, in which the British prevailed. There are differing estimates, but at least 20 million gallons of herbicides of varying components were sprayed to defoliate crops and trees during the Vietnam War. At least 12 million gallons, or 60%, of these herbicides were Agent Orange (AO), so named because of its striped orange storage barrels. Spraying was primarily done by specially equipped helicopters, or low-flying C-123s, under the call name

"Hades," and lasted from 1962 through 1971. This program named Operation Ranch Hand affected millions of acres in Vietnam, Laos and Cambodia. AO had two components including Tetrachloro-dibenzo-para-dioxin, and thought to be many times greater than the level approved by the United States Environmental Protection Agency. There were nine major producers of AO, most notably Dow and Monsanto. They claimed not to know the dangers of Dioxin. It is believed Dioxin can remain in humans for 11 to 15 years and in protected-from-sun soil for up to 100 years, and is not soluble in water. AO is no longer produced. Hundreds of thousands of Vietnam citizens and U. S. Vietnam veterans still suffer the effects of these extremely dangerous herbicides, especially AO. Vietnam veterans have a high incidence of health issues, such as throat cancer, liver diseases, Hodgkins' disease, lung cancer and colon cancer. Certain mental conditions, as well as birth defects, have also been detected and may be related to AO exposure.

The United States military dropped more bombs on North Vietnamese Army-occupied Eastern Laos during the Vietnam War than were dropped on Germany and Japan combined during WWII. There are still unexploded ordnances in large parts of those countries. The nature of the Vietnam War made it virtually impossible to know for sure, but the United States estimates that 200,000 to 250,00 South Vietnamese soldiers perished. Over 2,000,000 civilians, on both sides were killed. 58,000+ U. S. soldiers died and 304,000 were wounded. 1.1 million Viet Cong and North Vietnamese were killed, with thousands wounded. These figures include the Missing in Action. General Giap may have been right when he said, "It was a people's war."

In the Vietnam War, a commander was assigned a call name to distinguish from a radioman. My call name was "Waterbird" from my first mission to my last, no matter my location or mission. I hoped I would not have to use it, but I knew I would. I could not imagine completing many missions without having to call in a Prairie Fire or two. February 1968, was the first time I had been called "Waterbird." I was in the company of a couple of experienced SOG officers in an H-34 helicopter flying over Laotian mountain passes. They loved to show off to new members and subject them to theretofore-unknown fear. I was no exception. I sat with my feet close to the open side of the chopper, and watched tracers the size of footballs fly past, and smelled the trailing phosphorus disappear into the sky. "Waterbird," one of the officers yelled over the roar, "Better get back." There was no place to hide, so I backed up and prayed we did not go down. There were just the two SOG officers and me, and they had been through it more than a few times. They were laughing their heads off, but they quickly stopped laughing when a couple of 12.7mm rounds came too close to the chopper. I was genuinely scared, but these guys were not going to know it. No way in hell.

My role as Captain (Daiwi) was to command a

battalion of Nungs that could be as many as 1000, but mine numbered 200. Indigenous Nungs, Montagnards and Cambodes were CIA-recruited. Many Nungs had come to Vietnam from China's southern area of Kwangsi Province around the Highlands area of NV. The Montagnards were often referred to as hill people and "Yards." They did not particularly fight for money, but they were well paid by the United States government, under the auspices of the CIA. The Chinese Nungs had been exiled by Mao in the early 1950s, and worked primarily around the Ho Chi Minh Trail. They were sometimes called "indigs" and sometimes the "fat ones," although they were much smaller in stature than most U.S. soldiers. They hated the Vietnamese and the Chinese, and were hated in return. As a result, the Nungs were perfect to fight for the United States. Ferocious, fearsome, loyal, clever and brutal, they fought to the death. The bond between us quickly became very strong, due in part by necessity on both sides. The United States Army needed their trust, support and extremely good fighting abilities, and they needed our guidance and teaching. We had learned to communicate - they in broken English, and I in broken Vietnamese or Nung, facial expressions, hand gestures and a lot of initial frustration. Most of them could not count beyond three, and I was amazed at how fast they learned.

I consider myself a "universal" soldier. Obviously, I do not personally know every solider who served in our wars, but I respect their service more than

I can ever express. I identify with their struggles. I have had the same experiences, the same gnawing sickness and acute anxiety. I see the same devouring images and have the same thoughts that sometime make us nearly strangers to all who love and know us best. With my eyes wide open, in my sleep and nightmares, I see the faceless men with severed limbs, burns, and mental scars. I have felt the spit of disenchanted and ill-informed American citizens who blamed some of America's bravest for serving in the Vietnam War. Maybe, I think, this may have hurt more than anything else. I suppose they just could not understand or relate to what the soldiers had been through. I fought for their freedoms, or at least thought I did. If there is any fault, it does not lie with brave veterans, but with the government who sent them there. I would fight again if called upon, but would hope it is a war that should be fought and that our country goes in with the dedication needed to win it.

I awoke many mornings in Vietnam with the same conviction: *Fuck this. Go home.* But I was a soldier and a good one, and I knew there was only one way to fight a battle, even when the territory was internal like Vietnam: eyes wide open, straight ahead. *There is nothing left for me in New York anyway if I don't face this here.* I headed back to I Corps prepared to do whatever I needed to defeat the enemy.

My favorite quote about war comes from Nietzsche: "Nothing like a good war to make life so . . . personal." My Vietnam was so personal. I wrote my own rules while fighting in my enemy's backyard. I was a demigod in charge of everyone, already a servant to power. At times, however, I found myself a servant to powerlessness, too

When I began to write this autobiography, I chose not to write a "war" book. Instead, I chose to bring the reader into a world of privilege and into the pain, fear, and the impact of indelible memories before, during and after the hell of war. I included a few battles because I felt they were important to who I am and to the theme of the book. A few battles were major, some not, and some are merely incidental. With Vietnam far behind me, at least physically, I am still called Waterbird or Daiwi by a good number of my friends and acquaintances.

1.

PRIVILEGE, HEARTBREAK,
AND THINGS IN BETWEEN

I attended St. Luke's Private School in New Canaan, Connecticut. My father owned an apartment in New York City and we traveled back and forth until we moved into a Park Avenue high-rise in New York City when I was 12 or 13. I spent a lot of time as a young boy without a worry about the rest of my life. I lived high above the Manhattan streets and the never-ending noise, separated from the rank and file. I wore clothes from the best tailors, and frequented the best museums, and restaurants, where I ordered the best cuts of meat and received the best service from the maitre ds. I had tickets to the hottest Broadway shows and attended upper-crust schools. My classmates hailed from some of New York's wealthiest families.

Not considered a model kid by any stretch, I was still the impeccably dressed boy, with impeccable manners. I had been blessed with good looks, and that always made it a lot easier to attract girls. Outwardly, I was the boy that parents would have chosen to accompany their daughters to the homecoming dance. Inwardly, I wanted to be on the edge, always pushing, mentally anyway, to see how far I could go with my rebellion. New York City provided many outlets to push the adolescent envelope, but I escaped without getting into serious trouble. I credit my parents for that.

I come from a long line of Churches - 16 generations of pioneers, elders and gunslingers and tough guys from Boston to California by way of the Cumberland Gap, the Midwest Prairies and Death Valley. My ancestors' stories were broadcast on TV's "Death Valley Days" in the 50s. My mother, Charlene Church Pfeifer, loved me and I loved her. I looked more like her than my sister or brother. That made me proud because she was beautiful and sophisticated. A talented painter and interior decorator, she helped decorate the "SS United States," while working for Smyth, Urquhart & Marckwald. She was fun, and she made me laugh. Generous, loving and a firm believer in education, she and my Dad made sure I was well-schooled.

As a child in Connecticut, we had two pet goats and a Labrador Retriever. When mother called to us, "Come on kids, we are going for a ride," it was not unusual to climb into the car with mother and my siblings, and have one of the pet goats in the seat between us. That did not work too well with mother, but our Lab was with us a lot unless we were going to church. The dog usually had his head stuck out one of the side windows, its ears flopping in the wind. Occasionally, he would bark at the top of his lungs and could be heard for blocks. Mother did not care that people stared as she drove down the street with a dog's face stuck out the window. As I said, she made me laugh.

When I was 13, mother was diagnosed with ovarian cancer. I was heartbroken when she died, leaving me in a conflicted adolescence between new-found, and somewhat restricted, privileges. My life would never be the same. I acted up more than ever and got into lots of trouble with my father, Charles F. Pfeifer, a paper packaging executive, salesman, and a world-class hurdler. He commanded – in fact, demanded – respect. His advice for a successful life was "continuity" and he often said, "be bright, be brief, and be gone." My grandfather was a tough, but fair, New York City cop. In 1956, when I was 15, my father married Shirley Ewald, a member of the distinguished Ewald advertising family. Now, instead of just brother, Billie, and sister, Annie, I had two step-brothers, Theodore and Brewster (Bumpy) Loud. We never cultivated a close relationship in adolescence or in adulthood. Needing more discipline than my father and step-mother were able to provide, due in part to my cocky and semi-brilliant adolescent mind, I enrolled in Culver Military Academy in Culver, Indiana, when I was 15. I did not want to leave New York City. I loved it, but my father was a strict disciplinarian and I did what he said. Private school was, however, a tradition in my family, so I followed suit. I seriously considered attending Andover, but chose Culver, not so much because of its reputation, but because it also had a very good athletic program. Culver's football team played bigger schools from surrounding in-state cities and from Illinois and Ohio, and that appealed to me.

I did not have a lot of time to spend with my step-mother. I am sure she was not crazy about me and was probably relieved when I left for Culver. Thinking about it now, I, undoubtedly, resented her because she would never be the mother I had lost. She often left me behind at my grandparents' house while the family went on vacation or day trips because I had become too rebellious. Not fully understanding this, I vowed to get back at her in some way, somehow. Surely, I thought, I can think of something. That, of course, was my adolescent mind working overtime. I realized much later that she had done the best she could with a resentful boy, who obviously did not like her very much, but one who, nonetheless, called her mother. She helped me break into advertising with a great firm after I returned from my Vietnam tour.

Excelling in football and basketball at Culver, I was voted the best all-around athlete. Finishing Culver in 1959, I entered Dartmouth College and played football as a wide receiver and defensive back. I was eagerly looking forward to playing under the excellent tutelage and coaching of Bob Blackman for the next three years, but that did not happen. Dartmouth was great, but my time there was brief. My classmates and I engaged in a lot of arguing and fighting with Amherst boys. Nothing was personal. We liked most of the guys we met. Our arguments centered and escalated mostly over their invasion of our territory called "the all-girl Smith College." Testosterone flowed freely and we usually had a few too many beers before heading back to our dormitories after a night out. Usually, there were no problems, but one night I became a bit too controversial. I had a date with a beautiful Smith girl. I thought I would remember her name forever, but now it escapes me. We returned to her dorm an hour after curfew and her housemother was waiting at the door, her arms crossed over her chest and a pretty stern look on her face. I knew I was in trouble.

"Mr. Pfeifer, you are late bringing her back. Where have you been?" she demanded, reaching to wring one of my ears between her bony fingers.

"None of your damn business where I've been," I replied, attempting to leave.

"Mister," she exclaimed, "You stop right there. This most certainly is my business. I expect my girls to be in before curfew, and I do not condone their dates keeping them out late." She eyed me suspiciously, looking me straight in the eyes and moving a little closer to my face. "You've been drinking. Dean Dickerson will hear about this," she haughtily declared.

"And you can't wait to tell him," I sassed, pulling loose from her grip on my ear. Then, on a sudden whim, I dropped my trousers, brown-eyed her, and ran as fast as I could with my pants below my thighs.

My reputation was already badly tarnished, and this episode was quickly added to the stack of infractions. Dean Dickerson had heard plenty about my escapades and when this reached his very sharp ears, he had heard too much. Before he had the opportunity to talk to me however, I, with drunken delight, put a fire axe through a dorm door. I was summoned to his office promptly at 8:00 A.M. the next morning.

"Charles," Dean Dickerson sighed, leaning back in his chair. "I hardly know where to begin." He studied me for a minute or two, lips pursed, slowly shaking his head. I did not need to be told I was in deep trouble. The Dean chose his words carefully, making sure I understood the full impact.

"I am appalled to hear about your recent behavior, especially after what you pulled on Smith's housemother. She called me yesterday, and I don't have to tell you she was pretty upset. Violating curfew and being drunk are bad enough, but sassing the housemother and showing her your butt, or anyone else for that matter, are not acceptable behaviors. And how do you expect to pay for the dorm door you damaged? What do you have to say for yourself?"

"Not much, sir," I said meekly. "I got carried away."

"Yes sir, I believe you did." He paused for a moment, as I stood there squirming, hands behind my back and trying, without success, to hold my head high. He let me stand there shifting my feet for another minute or two. It seemed much longer. He was good at letting students have plenty of time to reflect about their infractions before passing judgment.

"Charles," he finally said again. "You have a lot of potential. You are smart and a very good athlete, yet you throw it away. You need to pull yourself together, and I do not believe you will be able to do that if you continue here. We expect students to conform to acceptable social norms and our rules. I am sad about what I have to do, but I have no choice. You have three options: I can expel you right now, you face possible jail time, or you can lend two precious years to Uncle Sam. Before you make a decision, would you like me to call your father?"

"Oh no, sir," I quickly replied. "I'll call him." I thought for only a moment. I might not have been a good student, but I was smart enough to know this was no contest. I had to answer to my Father, and if I had chosen anything other than Uncle Sam, I would have been in even greater trouble. "I'll choose Uncle Sam, sir," I responded meekly. I had not expected to be expelled, and I certainly did not want to go to jail for something as trivial as mooning Smith's housemother. The axe episode was a different matter, however. Two weeks later, Dartmouth was behind me and I reported to the Army training base at Fort Dix, New Jersey, where I played on the "Burros" football team as an end and defensive back.

What was supposed to be punishment and/or exile, for my Dartmouth behavior, turned out, ostensibly, to be a two-year "football scholarship." I loved my stint there, even though it was not all fun. A lot of hard work was involved, and I quickly learned discipline and respect. I can't say that my wildness was over, but I had begun to grow up, with still a long way to go.

After my stint at Fort Dix ended in 1960, I reported to Fort Benning, Georgia, and played football on its team, the "Doughboys," again as an end and defensive back. A football scout from West Point saw me play there, and thought I would make a good team member for West Point. He vetted and recommended me, and when my Father heard this, he called me. "Son, you are one lucky boy. You are considered a rogue student and this is a rogue student's ticket back into an Ivy League college. I will immediately arrange for the necessary recommendation letter." He could not wait to contact a Connecticut congressman, who wrote the letter and I was in. I reported to the United States Military Preparatory School at Fort Belvoir, where I studied until May 1961 and then moved on to West Point Military Academy in July 1961.

I played on the West Point football team under the coaching of Paul Dietzel and Dale Hall. West Point had a big-school schedule, such as Pitt, Penn State, Syracuse and, of course, its all-time rival, Navy. An injured shoulder, badly injured knees, and subsequent surgeries, knocked me out of football. However, even though I was sidelined with injuries, I was dressed and still part of West Point's team. The unquestioned highlight of my football career was the 65th Classic between the Army Black Knights and the Navy Midshipmen in November 1964. The game played out before a crowd of 100,000, including 2,700 cheering Cadets, in the John F Kennedy Stadium in Philadelphia. Carl Roland ("Rollie") Stichweh, Army's quarterback, was probably the greatest ground gainer in West Point history. Recently, he was inducted into the Army's Football Hall of Fame.

Every football fan knows that Roger Staubach, Navy's quarterback, went on to become one of the NFL's greatest. Both Stichweh and Staubach were seniors and badly wanted to go out as winners. Stichweh says of this 1964 game: "That win was the gift that keeps on giving for the decades that follow. It's a topic of discussion every time our old team gets together - and each play becomes greater every time we tell it."

In 1964, neither West Point nor Navy had ever won six in a row against the other. History has it at 30-30-5. Today, Navy leads the series at a 60-49-7. We all knew the 65th Classic would be hard-fought and tough, but we were ready. Staubach finished minus 22 on the day, and completed 12 of 20 passes for around 120 yards. A field goal decided the score: Army 11, Navy 8. "The Philadelphia Bulletin" reporter, Sandy Grady, wrote about that day: "Staubach joined "I-Spent-The-Day-On-My-Back-Quarterback Club." Have you ever heard the song, "There'll Be A Hot Time In The Old Town Tonight?"

I had been a mediocre cadet at West Point, graduating at the top of the bottom third of my class. I was smart enough to graduate with a better record, but I had difficulty focusing on academics. I still wanted to have a good time within the confines of the West Point community, so I did just what I needed to graduate, but that was it. The only people to whom I had endeared myself were my cohorts in crime. Sometimes accompanied by my friend and fellow cadet, Bobby

Jones, I spent a lot of hours walking back and forth with a rifle on my shoulder, called "walking the area," West Point's punishment for demerits and offenses against the rules. Some cadets were punished with confinement, except for visits to the bathroom, the library and for meals, so there were others worse than me. Because of my injuries, I didn't have the opportunity to live up to my potential in sports, but it was great while it lasted.

I could never have imagined a time when I would realize that being privileged might be a mirage. I did not know that privilege does not, nor can it, provide insulation from the vicissitudes of life. I would not discover that until much later. Actually, I am not sure if my life's experiences have been destiny, or if they simply hinged on the choices I made. Had I known what those choices embodied, I would have been a bit more discriminating and a lot more careful. I would have changed a lot of things and now wonder why I did them, especially mooning the housemother. I did not care about showing my butt, but it certainly was not a polite thing to do. I had been reared better. When my parents heard about it, they were horrified. I chalked it up to adolescence.

I got a letter from a West Point players got a letter from a West Point football player, which moved me:

"My *name is Drew Hennessy (#73) and I am a firstie right tackle on the Army football team. I am writing to you today because we share the same home state, beautiful New York, and both represented the greatest team in this nation. One of the proudest accomplishments of my life was my entrance into the Army football brotherhood and being able to represent this nation and my brothers before me. Although you are no longer on the fields of Michie, (outdoor stadium on the campus of the U. S. Military Academy in West Point) your influence and spirit still lies within the heart of this football team. I firmly believe that there is no stronger bond in this country than the Army football brotherhood and the relationship we as players form both on and off the field. As my brother, and my fellow believer in this team, I promise to give my heart and soul to this team so that you are still represented. I vow to honor those before me and carry out the winning tradition that embodies this group and this institution. We as a team will no longer settle for anything less than success and when we finally attain that goal, we will have your presence in our hearts. I hope that you enjoy this season as we go forth and honor the values that this brotherhood was founded on. Please keep on believing in this team and this strong brotherhood."*

This letter is the genesis for the instincts and discipline that make a good combat officer.

2.

RANGER TRAINING, FORT BENNING

As a West Point graduate, I was required to spend four years in the military. After a 60-day leave, I reported again to Fort Benning in 1966, to begin my Ranger training. I figured what the hell. I had a great time there before. It did not take me too long to find out this time would be a whole lot different.

Ranger School is widely recognized as one of the toughest combat training and mentally challenging in the world and the Army. Ranger training encompasses three phases: Camp Darby at Fort Benning, Georgia, Camp Merrill, in the remote mountains near Dahlonega, Georgia, and finally Camp Rudder in Florida, at Elgin Air Force Base. All three Ranger training phases are designed to test the physical stamina, mental toughness and leadership abilities of the candidates. Always testing and pushing myself to the utmost limits, I mustered up every bit of my mental and physical strengths. Still, there were a few times I seriously doubted if I had it in me. However, I was determined to be the best and I was deadly serious about mastering all that was thrown my way. One of the most important mental things I had to learn was to think fast on my feet. Anything that smacked of either fear or acute anxiety might have eliminated me from Ranger school, so I was able to keep those feelings in check. The "Water Phase" was the most difficult for me. It consisted of various water exercises in conditions that are similar to actual enemy situations. Without a doubt, Ranger School is a tough nut, and I greatly respect all who finish the course. Estimates show that roughly 50% to 60% of Ranger candidates, despite their earlier training, do not complete the entire course for a number of reasons. Sometimes, it all comes down to a simple matter of personality, physical and mental stamina, or in-team politics.

My fellow soldiers comprised a varied background: Navy Seals, new recruits, and men from other branches of service. Some of us thought we were giving our Commanders a hard time when they instructed, "Drop and give me 20 push-ups. On the ground." We yelled, in unison, "Did you say give you 50, Sarge?" The Commanders pasted on an indifferent look that I later learned to master. Oh yeah, we were really giving them a hard time. Indifference was not the right word. Looking back, I realized the instructors had to be thinking, "I have to be hard-nosed as hell, because I know what these little bastards are going to face. No way am I going to show them my softer side."

At Fort Benning, I met John Wilbur, Yale man and Navy Seal. He spent 18 months in Vietnam, first in Demolition Team 22 and Seal Team 2, in the Mekong Delta, and was a Purple Heart recipient. He became the Chief Assistant U. S. Attorney for the American Virgin Islands. We became fast friends and stayed in frequent touch until his death in 2013.

The ground and the tower stages of the United

States Army Airborne School (Jump School) were the easiest parts of training for me, even though my already-injured knees and legs bore the impact of the repetitive simulated jumps.

Even though close-to-the-ground jump training was very thorough, I was always somewhat apprehensive as I climbed into a C-123 or C-130 to do static line jumps, particularly the first one. I gave myself a pep talk as the plane took off, but subsequent jumps never really got any better. The familiar adrenaline rush was always with me. Not fear exactly, but close. I tried never to show that anxiety, however. As the plane rose to 1000 to 1500 or so feet, and the Jump Master yelled, "Stand Up, Hook Up, Shuffle to the Door, and Go! Go! Go!" I was out of one of the plane's two doors with nothing beneath. Although in the company of others, I was on my own, floating to the drop zone, trusting the chute would open, hoping for a soft landing and rehearsing in my mind all I had been taught. I can do this.

Earning my wings in the required five jumps, I wanted to move on to Master Wings, but that would be in the future. That would take a lot more jumps. Along the way, I found I did not have the inclination to complete the required jumps. I have done about 10 free falls in a non-combat setting. Athough not being much of a praying man, free falling made me a believer, at least until I touched down on terra firma.

Named Class Leader at Ranger and Airborne Schools, I received the Top Ranger Award. There was a huge and spectacular presentation ceremony in the company of about 400 battalion Rangers and an eclectic mix of military men from all branches of the service for those of us who had successfully completed Ranger training. The Ranger Tab on my shoulder was the crowning highlight.

I was ready, physically and emotionally, to confront and dispatch whatever enemy came my way and to "give" my life for my country, if needed. I was not yet cognizant that "giving" my life should have been more like "I will allow Uncle Sam to borrow me for a while and if the interest he has to pay me for that loan could result in the loss of my life, I will fight like hell to save it, or I will die like a man." Ranger candidates are now required to finish additional training, designed to root out less-qualified soldiers. In mock POW conditions, they are subjected to mistreatment almost to the breaking point. Being able to withstand whatever torture they might encounter as a prisoner was crucial, as was proficiency in the use of weapons, scuba diving, navigation and parachuting. They are taught escape, evasion, survival techniques and how to keep one step ahead of the enemy in every phase of warfare.

All our special talents were honed, and all were cross-trained. There was no operation that every successful Ranger could not do. The cadre acted and thought as one. We escaped additional training that was added some time later.

I found my destiny and encountered my true roots

there - clan Campbell, not Park Avenue types, Ivy Leaguers, or West Pointers, but my Scotch-Irish brethren, the rank and file who colonized America and went on, rich or poor, to lead America's military ranks for generations. I was a man born for unconventional warfare.

My military and life destinies were sealed at Fort Benning without my full recognition, and nearly without a second thought. They would be difficult, dangerous, and life changing, ending with physical and mental challenges I would be fighting to overcome all my life.

After Fort Benning and another leave in 1967, I received my first duty assignment as a minted Airborne Ranger. My orders to report to Schweinfurt, Germany, were confusing in their military language, but I was finally on my way to places and things I could not even imagine.

3.

SCHWEINFURT, GERMANY

In 1967, I was a First Lieutenant assigned to a mechanized infantry unit, part of the Third Division, in Schweinfurt, in the German State of Bavaria, on the right side of the Main River. At its peak, about 11,000 American troops and family members called it home. Although the Schweinfurt base did not play a major role in the war, it was there on a stand-by basis, if needed. One of the first things I saw was "Ledward Barracks" over the arched entryway. My first thought was that the building looked like a prison.

The countryside was beautiful, but I was not fond of this unexciting and dull assignment. It was boring, and the barracks did turn out to be a sort of prison and I could not wait to get out. Working in the motor pool as a greasemonkey and performing mundane tasks in and around the barracks were not what I came into the Army to do. I was ready for some blood and guts action. Before my career was over, I would have plenty.

My combat training was never over: Morning to evening, and sometimes at night. When the colors came down, though, I headed to town in my Jaguar XKE, ready for some fun with the beautiful German girls.

After inspection one Saturday morning, Gerry Ogier, a close friend then and now, and I were in the Officers' Club nursing a drink and watching out the big plate glass window as paratroopers practiced jumps. I looked at Gerry. "Do you think they would let me do a jump just for the hell of it?"

"Why not? Are you sure you want to though? A couple of drinks can alter a jump," he warned.

"I know, I know," I argued. "I'll be fine." I approached the Non-Combat Commander. "How about grabbing a static line?"

"Sure," he said. " Load up."

Floating down was amazing until I realized I could not control the chute enough to keep from landing on the hood of a truck, inflicting a huge dent. The chute split down the middle, and I bounced off the truck and hit the ground hard. Although not badly hurt, it knocked the breath out of me and I was plenty shook up. I laid still for a minute, and Gerry came running. "I'm okay," I laughed, getting up. "Just got the air knocked out of me."

"Laugh," he said, half angry, "go ahead and laugh. You just scared the hell out of me." Back inside, we grabbed another drink. I headed for a slot machine, and my last yank on the handle yielded a fifty-buck jackpot. "We're going downtown!" I yelled over at Gerry. Downtown, we had a few more drinks and finally headed home in Gerry's brand new Volvo. The trip was not very far, but it was far enough for a German national to run a red light and T-bone the Volvo, bending it nearly in two. We both saw the car coming and knew we were going to be hit, but it was too late to get out of the way. Miraculously, we did not get a scratch. However, the Volvo was not as lucky; it was totaled. A few more inches one way or the other, and we would have been killed. We had given a buddy a ride home, and he was asleep, or maybe passed out, in the back seat. Grinding metal and a gigantic jolt awakened him in a heartbeat. He jerked up, rubbing his eyes with his fists "What the holy hell was that?" he exclaimed, as he attempted to crawl out a rear window. It had been another interesting day.

When I took the thorough and rigorous four-day test involving long runs, map reading, compass reading, rope and tactical training, I was in superb physical shape. Confident the test would be no problem, I passed with the highest grade and was awarded the Expert Infantry Badge. No favorites were played. We were all the same in the eyes of the commanders. Being long past ready to move on for more exciting duty, I had made a request for transfer before taking the final test, and the Colonel ultimately granted my transfer, and I moved on to Bad Tolz, Germany. Even though my time at Schweinfurt was short, I still remember some good times there. The "Call to Colors" sounded for the last time in September 2014, when the base was officially closed and turned over to the German government.

4.

BAD TOLZ, GERMANY

I was assigned to the 10th Special Forces Group, based in Bad Tolz, Germany, where the incomparable and beautiful Alps loomed in the background. Big tough guys from all over Europe came there to train in 1967 and 1968. The intense and thorough training seemed never-ending: dawn-to-dusk, weapons training, climbing and parachute jumps. On one of our night jumps, the pilot mistook city lights for our inverted "L" landing zone. One of my buddies landed on an unfortunate homeowner's chimney and laid there swaying in the wind attempting to untangle himself. Finally, the homeowners, having heard the thud, ran out to see what caused the commotion and helped him to the ground. I landed back-to-back with a hay rake — one of those big ones with huge wheels and about 20 feet wide. "Shit!" I exclaimed, lying quiet for a couple of minutes while assessing my condition and feeling foolish. I do not know where the rest of my unit landed, but everyone was safe, either by sheer luck or expertise. There were some surprised people on the ground. I have had some near misses, and a good bit of fear in my jumps, but no serious injuries. I thought back on my unfortunate jump in Schweinfurt, Germany, hoping, but not believing, I would never have to do another jump. I conquered most, if not all, of my anxiety about jumping, but I was never able to dispel it completely.

Through a mutual friend, I became acquainted with Ernst Von Stade, a German Count. He invited me to his home, where we shot birds and skeet. A gracious host and gentlemen, he often invited me as his guest to attend Munich's opera house. He liked me, he said, because I was a "high bred" American, an alpha male and Special Forces. He was impressed, and I enjoyed his company. We philosophized about war, and he recounted his uncle's experience while fighting in Russia during WWII. He said he bore no animosity about former enemies. "It was simply black and white," he said. I knew what he meant. After my return home, he and his wife visited me in New York. They loved our City, and I was proud to introduce them to it.

My commanding officer at Bad Tolz recognized my potential and probably liked me personally - maybe a little of both. Our unit needed a highly-trained officer, not just for counter-insurgency situations, but also in water specialties. He sent me to Greece for two months of intense and difficult water training. I swam for long distances and was yanked out of the water by high-speed boats with side loop arrangements. This was not fun, nor easy, but it was necessary. I wondered if my commanding officer at Bad Tolz liked me as I thought, or actually hated me and found a way to inflict punishment.

I practiced demolition work on distant islands with Georgios Panagoulis, a highly-trained Greek Army Special Forces soldier, with great leadership abilities. He became a new friend, and often invited me to dinner with him and his generous and gracious mother. After dinner and some polite conversation, Georgios would rise from his chair, kiss his beloved mother on the forehead, and say to me, "Come on, let's go to Asteria Beach, flirt with the girls and have a few more drinks." I was always ready for that. I admired Georgios, loved and accepted him as someone who would be a life-long friend. He spent a lot of his childhood during the Axis occupation of Greece in World War II on the Ioian Island of Lefkada. In spite of his skills and training, he was killed in a training accident about a year after I met him. I was curious about his unnecessary death, and think it may have been related to his brother's activities in opposition to the Regime of the Colonels. His brother was also killed in a suspicious car crash, widely believed and accepted as having been caused, as well, by the ruling Colonels.

My on-the-job Special Forces training continued throughout Europe. During time off and weekends I traveled to Switzerland to see a girlfriend, always returning to Bad Tolz.

5.

TO DA NANG

In January 1968, I was on my way to active duty in Da Nang. "Stop milling around, maggots. Give me a company formation," a Marine Sgt. yelled. "Three platoons right here." I knew a lot of my mischief was over and that I was in for some real combat. Preparing to board the C-130 Blackbird for the flight out of Saigon, I made sure my Green Beret was sitting just right. Very early, I acquired a habit of checking my Beret. I had been soundly chastised when I first arrived at SOG headquarters in Saigon *wearing* the Beret. "We are a *secre*t organization, solider. Take that Beret off your head right now."

I eyed the Rio-tanned Braniff stewardesses in ochre Emilio Pucci skirts standing on the stairs of a pink, blue and green Braniff 707 over at the next gate where the fresh Marines were loading. We were all on our way to Da Nang, but I doubted we would see each there there. Now accustomed to the familiar and recurring scene, the stewardesses dolefully observed the Marine kids. Braniff chartered many planes for the war effort, and the stewardesses knew the hell these kids would face. One pointed at the Blackbird, and the others began talking, laughing and looking over at us. Maybe, I thought, she was telling them what assholes we were or maybe explaining what a Blackbird meant in Vietnam. I thought if they knew about us, it was damned sure the Viet Cong did. I hoped the stewardesses were merely flirting, and I flirted back. Except for the odd nurse or nun, I would not see another white woman until I came back to Saigon and Bangkok afterward.

The unmarked Blackbird C-130, with a bellyful of cargo, flew out of Saigon headed for Da Nang. The C-130 was the Project used to transport our materials. It was a basic milk-run. Aboard were just two Taiwanese civilian pilots in mirrored Ray-Bans and plain clothes, and a blond civilian "crew chief" and me. I thought the crew chief might be a former football player by the looks of him, if I was any judge, and I considered myself pretty much of an expert on football. He was just a good old-fashioned Langley man with a boilerplate, company-issued heart of stone. For no good reason, which he hadn't divulged to me, he had me sit out the dark flight "alone" in the cargo bay. I was strapped to a windowless cargo seat atop four deafening turbo props. I also figured he did not like me or resented me, and wanted me to know, at least for a short time, that he was in charge. Maybe it was none of the above, but I did not like it. On floor-length pallets beside me were crates of sabotaged Communist China mortar rounds for our enemy's 82-mm that would explode when used. Ours were 81-mm weapons. The NVA cut their ordnance a millimeter wider than ours, so they could use our captured rounds, while theirs wouldn't fit in our barrels.

Just fuckin' great! Just one piece of live shrapnel

or one tracer hitting one of those pallets and I would be on the next plane of existence as flotsam on the China Sea, blown to oblivion. I began to sweat. "That's Happy Valley," the crew chief yelled over the roar of turbo props and ordnance concussion as I humped my gear down the Blackbird's ramp onto the Da Nang Airstrip.

Whump! Whump! Whump!

"Sounds like the Marines are in a world of shit," the crew chief yelled. "What else is new?" I give him a nasty look just to let him know I did not appreciate one bit being left in the back of that flight. It was a chicken-shit, and totally unnecessary, two-hour entombment, in which he seemed to take pleasure. I was not pleased about being left (for security reasons he said, of all things) on that empty lane of storage airstrip, with no convoy in sight and I certainly did not care to hear about the U.S. Marines being in a world of shit spoken of lightly. I have always been a fan of the Marines except in certain circumstances, and I was scared shitless myself. The concussions made my skin crawl.

"Give 'em hell, you fuckers!" the crew chief yelled again, all gung-ho as the ramp rose with a jerk. He looked just like Cecil B. DeMille on a crane, barking garbage for the action shot, the beginning of my contempt for civilian espionage types in Vietnam. "Someone will be by in a few minutes," he said. Actually, it was a full hour before I was picked up and driven to FOB-4 for processing. He gave me a runway salute before stepping back into the Blackbird. As the

41

huge plane taxied off, I flipped a salute of my own, which I was sure, or hoping, he would see. I saw nothing but black, one-way spy windows screwed into the back of a painted black, unmarked 100-foot, 50-ton airplane, the U.S. Government's attempt at hiding its presence, which was front and center. It was not exactly a braggadocio mentality, although there was a bit of that. I thought what good is a need-to-know-basis if you cannot tell everyone. It was more of a psychological warfare: *We are here in your shitty little country 'cause we have to be, responding to your espionage with our own, except we are too big to hide.*

The emptiness of the airstrip told me Da Nang was nothing like Saigon, even though I acknowledged that no place could ever be. There was not a soul in sight in the first row of this theatre of mass destruction playing out to the west. Behind me lay a parched, hazy stretch of sandy loam, clearly not far from water. Standing there for just a moment or two, I quickly scanned the airstrip. I noted that hangers, planes, jeeps, trucks, and cargo bays lined both sides of the runway. The Marines were in a "pile of shit" after all, and in a few minutes I would witness, both mentally and physically, all the evidence I needed.

Whump! Whump! Whump!

Another pair of Phantom 4s took off to the east, circled over the water and dropped their payload on Happy Valley. I saw the target zone then, too large to recognize at first. The planes were literally taking a grid square off the map, the end of history for that particular plat. I envisioned what it must have looked like in the Briefing Room at the Tactical Control Center, or on the acetate transparency the bombadier doubtless had over his lighted target board.

Whump! Whump! Whump!

I heard dull thuds a few miles off. More high explosives, except this time, black smoke arose in neat columns at the near perimeter of the grid-square. My first whiff of napalm came shortly after the impact of concussion.

Whump, whump, whump

I felt it in the balls of my heels, vibrating up through my spine like a big whack to the back of my head, not just once, but every time. Technically, it was painless, but if pain is pressure on the nervous system, the thuds were worse. This was my welcome to the Vietnam War and the Da Nang Airstrip. Every instinct and my training told me to get into the first building I saw. A sliding overhead door was open enough to get through without the indignity of having to crawl under. I searched for light switches, and found none. I was in a building with little visibility, and no one in sight. *What kind of a welcome is this?* Soon I learned there were a number of things and men a whole lot more important than I, or the welcome I had received.

Another round of ordnance concussed, followed by the unmistakable belching of a Vulcan Cannon. I made my way a few yards farther in and lit up a Camel. The match glow was enough to show me I was not alone at all: Aluminum boxes, stacked like cordwood, rose from floor to ceiling. While aluminum is hard to associate with coffins, the size and shape of these made it obvious and left no that I had crawled into the base morgue with men who, a short time ago, had been fighting for their country and their lives and lost. I was damn sure I was going to do all I could not to join them. "Holy Hell!" I cursed under my breath. I approached the boxes, tentatively at first, then faster, as if drawn to them by some unknown force. I suppose it was curiosity, but I cannot imagine why I would be curious. I already knew who they were: My forebears.

Sgt. Bobby-Joe Morris A Co 2/7 USMC. By a dying match-light, I read the tag aloud, and struck another match to read the tags on coffins above and below, and then a few more from the next stack. Again and again, they were two-part Appalachian names, *Joe-Earl, Billy-Ray*, good ole' boys culled from that right-angle grid on the American map that's always provided the best soldiers and football players: down the northeast corridor through Pennsylvania, Kentucky, Tennessee and Georgia to the Florida Panhandle, across the Cumberland Gap all the way through to El Paso. *Drink all night and shoot the ass out of a squirrel at the crack of dawn.* Advantaged soul I had become, though, the sight of the names made me feel like Louis XVI, his neck on the same guillotine used for the procession of commoners. *Is it just a matter of time for me?* After my eyes adjusted to the dim light, I saw that the stacks kept on going. I started to tally them, but it somehow seemed vulgar, and I stopped. There were so many. I was overcome with sadness. What a waste of men. The first few I wondered: *Where did you get it? Did you have any chance? Did you blow it? Was it bad luck? Did the guy next to you get it, too, or was it just your day?* I stopped wondering and took it all in, realizing there was a combination of answers. These U.S. Marines, 200 or 300 of them, bagged, and tagged, were going home, not under the warm gaze of a sympathetic stewardess, but alone, in the cargo bay of a C-141, where loved ones waited and grieved.

I had become part of Project Eldest Son on the flight to Da Nang without a clue what I would be called upon to do. Project Eldest Son was one of the most secret plans ever approved by the U. S. Joint Chiefs of Staff, and perhaps one of the most effective and typical SOG responses to NVA cunning. SOG would get onto a back pass of the Ho Chi Minh Trail and leave stacks of "Friendly Fire" in strategic places. The self-exploding ammunition was made in Okinawa for this project, and was camouflaged to look a few months or years old. If we got lucky, some sandbagged NVA mortar-teams would be blown up. I have no way of knowing how many succumbed to this ammo, but I believe it was quite a few. I came across the vague remains of four men who had probably been such a team. Certain they were safe, they had bunkered down by the banks of the Perfume River. They never knew what hit them.

Alone on the Song Cai River planting caches of exploding fake ammunition rounds, I had to envision some rationale for it being in the spot I chose, any scenario the enemy could buy into. I secured the ammo under a filigrce of garbage to resemble spent ammo, transplanted foliage, and a period's worth of earth. I have never again felt, as when planting those rounds, that strange mixture of precision, creativity and terror: *brown earth, green plants, green mortars, brass bullets, and goose bumps.* The job had to be done quickly and efficiently. I moved as fast as possible, but it felt like slow motion - somewhat like coming into a pitch-dark building in the early morning when all is quiet and you cannot see a thing. Someone or something is behind you, and you cannot move fast enough to get behind closed doors to safety.

I was transformed by a change in diet, needing to be very protective about leaving spores on Eldest Son operations. I had eaten nothing but rice and fish for days before I was to plant the ammo. There could be no "American" smell if, per chance, I had to take a dump within a kilometer of the place. Nouc mam (dipping sauce) would stink for days afterwards. I prayed my luck would hold, and it did. I was not afraid of dying, but of what might come before. I could only envision how bleak the NVA would make my final days if they caught me there. I had my moments. Many times I trembled by the riverside at twilight and thwarted my desire to inhale cigarette smoke and blow smoke rings into the hot and stifling air. I was the only white man for 100 kilometers and the smell of smoke filtering through the haze of the jungle would have given me away. Sometimes, I felt safe enough to let the Nungs toss grenades into the water to kill fish, which they ate raw. The American men ate long-range patrol packets: Dry food mixed with water tasted pretty good. We all, particularly the Nungs, missed being able to smoke. They loved squatting, their asses pulled up between their knees, puffing away on cigarettes and watching the smoke drift away.

My senses were always on high alert and would remain so for the War's duration. I had no idea I had come home and that the rest of the world would forever seem foreign. I had heard that a newborn takes in more new data in his first year than in the rest of his life combined, and my first half-hour in Da Nang was a similar baptism. I had not yet gotten it, but I had learned four of Vietnam's great lessons: *New dimensions of pain from the Phantoms' thuds, new ways of feeling alone and vulnerable, first in the Blackbird, then being alone on this airstrip, and new ways at looking at life, history, and ontology.* Watching that grid square disappear, I learned, at last, the self-awareness that comes with a 24-hour self-appraisal gut-check, and that brute-force honesty that peacetime can never know.

6.

FIRST MISSIONS AND
THE CHAIN COMMAND

In mid-January, 1968, right after my arrival in Da Nang, I experienced my first self-assigned mission. I ordered two AH-1 Cobra gunship attack helicopters on standby at FOB-4 off to Gunoi Island, south of Marble Mountain, where the stacks of the dead were stored and the ground was damp with blood. Coordinating with a Major of the First Amphibious Marines, around 50 of my Nungs and I, together with the Marines, spent some time attacking reinforced NVA positions in the area.

Enemy fire was increasing to the north, and I organized a company-size mission to take on the Viet Cong, who were getting very bold in and around Marble Mountain. I lost a First Sergeant to a mine, even though we were able to blow up their bunkers and clear positions. The Viet Cong were Communist guerilla fighters. Although not members of the NVA, they were, nonetheless, supported by it. When we began to evacuate the area South of Marble Mountain, I noted signs that the Viet Cong had returned. I realized I had succumbed to conventional warfare, very much a losing proposition there. The Da Nang area itself was beginning to feel quite unsafe. I felt unnerved and began implementing additional security measures.

Mad Mike Rollinson and I flew to Saigon for debriefing, made the rounds of the bars and brothels, and our moods got dark. We crossed paths with Pulitzer-winning "Life" photographer, Cathy Leroy, a well-known leftist and, I suspected, sympathizer of the NVA, some of whom she interviewed at the Hue Citadel. She glanced at us as we passed, but I just could not let it go, not liking her looks or her politics. After a few words, I pointed my snub-nose .38 revolver at her. In parting, I picked her up by the ankles and held her upside down. She screamed and yelled for help, and I finally dropped her. With more nasty looks, she hastily departed. I never saw her again, nor did I want to.

Mike and I were drunk and getting more so by the minute, increasingly upset by the manipulation and conniving of local maitre-ds and madams. It came to a head in a rooftop whorehouse/bar. We decided to get back some of the money we had spent in Saigon, and we held up the place at gunpoint, netting around $2,500.00. Outside, we stole a Jeep, raced toward the SOG safe house at the airport, and were stopped by the MPs, because it was after curfew. I was not exactly going the speed limit. Being Special Forces, however, we were merely escorted to the safe house.

Later that night, two senior SOG Sergeants from II Corps awakened us. Covered in blood, they told us they just killed a Saigon cab driver that had held them up at gunpoint. We bedded them down for the night, and told them not to worry because one would ever know who did the deed. Next morning, Mad Mike and I put the stolen Jeep into the C-130 Blackbird for a flight back to Da Nang, where it became FOB-4 property in the possession of Colonel Overby. No one asked where the jeep came from, and we were not about to divulge that information.

A week later, I was in the planning stage of a mission to Thong Duc. A Marine Lieutenant, who had flipped to the enemy side, had been brainwashed, or under some other circumstance, was running a NVA POW camp at the site of a former CIDG (Civilian Irregular Defense Group). The CIDG was set up by the CIA to counter expanding Viet Cong (rebel) influence in South Vietnam's Central Highlands. Small teams of the United States Army Special Forces moved into villages and set up Area Defense Centers. They focused on local defense and civic action, training and arming villagers. Preferably, we wanted to capture the POW Marine, or that failing, kill him. Without having to use any imagination, we knew that where we would probably find him would be the last place an American pilot wanted to go down.

The mission would be intense and personal because I was on my own. It was also impersonal because I did not know this guy or even his name, although I learned he knew mine. How I did not know. I sat at the table with my commanding officers mapping out the strategy as though it was an everyday occurrence. I argued with myself about both the moral and personal aspects of the mission. I was going to kill someone who a relatively short time ago was one of us. *What happened to make him shift positions? Did he reach the same crossroads that I am about to reach?*

Did he argue with himself about his decision? Was he forced into it by becoming a prisoner and having to do whatever it takes to survive? We would be in Laotian territory where we weren't supposed to be, but we had to get the SOB. I had never killed face-to-face, but this mission might require me to do that. What if we encountered the turncoat Marine in close quarters, which I guessed we probably would, and I was the one who had to do the job? Even if it turned out I was not the one who had to pull the trigger, I would be responsible. I would have to give the order. There was no way around it, and I accepted that.

All my training had brought me to this point, and my military countenance kicked in. I put on the familiar face of infallibility and courage that I now wore most of the time. It was part of me and I would do whatever I had to do. I had taken the Oath. I heard the commanders. "We send in our recon team and hope it can give the intelligence we need to go in fast and get out fast. The team can tell us what numbers of the NVA we will have to deal with, preferably annihilate, before our mission can be accomplished. It will literally be touch and go."

I quickly learned that as soon as my team was on the way to get the culprit that made the mission necessary in the first place, I was totally alone and on my own. It was just me and my team, in which I had to place the utmost trust. This was my mission, and I was the Captain, the commander-in-chief. The ultimate arbiters of my life were not the name, rank or serial numbers of the Geneva Convention, the Army or my oath to God, Duty and Country. They were, instead, as Walter Brennan, Dean Martin and Ricky Nelson, sing ad nauseum on the CIDG jukebox, "my team, my weapons and me." There was nothing, or no one else. It was rather like having all the weapons you need hanging on the wall where good ole Kentucky boy and friend, Sergeant Rawlings, kept his guns, but when the ultimate test comes, when you have no choice but to use your weapons, will it come together as a success or failure? It was all in my hands. I was an elite solider, MACVSOG Special Forces now, and I, call name Waterbird, was the commanding unit officer. All my training must now come to bear on whatever enemy, if any, we found below us, across some river from us, or facing us. It was my duty. It was now up to me, totally irreversible, and I realized that the chain of command in Vietnam was more relative than I could ever have imagined. I knew my elite and thorough training had made me as knowledgeable and capable as anyone could possibly be. Now, it was up to me to do or die. I could "do."

We searched unsuccessfully, and senior officers finally scrubbed the mission about which I had been so apprehensive. I did not need to guess why. I was disappointed, but I understood that the NVA far outnumbered us and the mission had a big chance of failing. I never learned the fate of the Marine, who, early on, made me question myself, my morals, my responsibility, and indeed, my country. I chose my country. There was no other choice. I was not a coward or a soldier who would not fulfill his military oath to the best of his ability. Whether the Marine was dead or alive did not much concern me. Either way was okay, as it was, undoubtedly, better for everyone concerned. He probably was paying, or had already paid, a high price for being there, just like the rest of us.

7.

KHAM DUC AND KHE SANH

Kham Duc was an isolated Special Forces Camp just inside the South Vietnam border with Laos. Then it was known as the Quang Tin Province, now Phuoc Son District. In the event a rescue mission needed to be launched, I spent a lot of time there with the Nungs I commanded.

Here, I met and befriended Lieutenant James W. McElroy, Launch Site Commander at Kham Duc. It did not take much time before we became partners in crime. James had a terrific sense of humor, but no one dared cross him. When it came to duty, he was a "no nonsense" commander. He served two tours in Vietnam and received a Bronze Star for valor. To say that we enjoyed each other's company would be an understatement, and we became life-long friends. Just about every evening, at the end of a long day, he came looking for me. "Come on," he urged "Let's go to town." He did not have to coax me. So just about every night we drank, "tested" weapons like grenades, M-60 machine guns and light anti-tank weapons. One evening after a long and arduous day, we loaded our projector with the film "Bonnie and Clyde" and watched until we gleaned that it was a subversive anti-war film. McElroy yelled, "Stop the projector! I am not watching any more of that trash." For a man with too much to drink, he moved quickly. He was across the room in a flash and grabbed the film and we both pissed on it and filled it with CAR-15 bullets. I pulled my lighter from my pocket and built a fire with all three reels.

Most mornings, I ran track with James on Kham Duc's small airstrip, aware that at any time our sworn enemies had us in their gun barrels' crosshairs. Knowing that there was an open-ended $5,000.00 to $10,000.00 price on our heads, we still felt reasonably safe. If any shots were fired, all hell would be unleashed upon the heads of the perpetrators. These fighters were not only ferocious, but smart, as well. They knew better than start something they had no chance of finishing. I still had that destiny to fulfill, and so far I had been a very lucky man.

The last week in April I choppered out of Kham Duc at twilight to join my reinforced company of 160 Nungs in Phu Bai, on the way to north of the Tri-Border area of Laos, Cambodia, and Vietnam, always a hotly-contested staging area. Our recon-in-force mission, code-named Tennessee Valley, was to gauge enemy activity in the Trail area and destroy targets of opportunity. At dusk, five days into the mission, I sent Lt. Blatherwick and a 20-man platoon to recon a hill on which we had been steadily advancing. Blatherwick shortly radioed back that it was covered with enemy. I ordered him to take them under fire, and then called into the Forward Air Controller for an air strike. It was only when I heard "Roger, Waterbird. ETA 15 minutes," that I realized the magnitude: For the first time in my life, I was in a unit-command position, totally responsible for close to 100 men. I got my first sense of omnipotence – even exhilaration - when I saw the A-4s swooping down and leveling the entire hill in less than two minutes. In a few more minutes, the wave of A-4s was followed by the deafening whine of Napalm strikes. The next day we mounted what was left of the hill and found only a few "crispy critters," plus the blood spores of more casualties. This was my first sense that these dedicated and fierce fighters were, in their own way, quite elite and just as loyal to their men and to their cause as we were. They did not leave their dead behind even under heavy fire.

Between May 10 and May 12, 1968, shortly after I left Kham Duc for one of my shorter missions in Khe Sanh and Phu Bai, the 2nd NVA Division overran the camp and many close friends were lost when a C-130 carrying 100 Montagnards and U. S. personnel was shot down. Many varying accounts have been written about this extremely fierce battle. Most accounts are quite accurate, according to history.

In late April 1968, two recon team leaders, and I, were in Khe Sanh, a major Marine outpost in northwestern South Vietnam, with Laos to the west, the DMZ and North Vietnam, just to the north. The base was designed to block North Vietnamese incursions, making it strategic to the U. S. and the North Vietnamese Army. The United States could prevent NVA infiltration into South Vietnam and cut off a main enemy supply and communication route, the Ho Chi Minh Trail. Also, General Westmoreland, who was in charge of military operations there, hoped to launch an invasion into Laos and cut off the Trail.

The base was surrounded by hills quite a distance apart. With their elephant grass, bamboo thickets, and uninhabitable jungle, they provided perfect cover from which the enemy could launch a major attack. In late December 1967, or early 1968, intelligence reported the arrival of several PAVN Divisions within striking distance of Khe Sanh Command Base. The Marines moved in, and on January 20, 1968, a PAVN defector alerted Colonel David Lownds that an attack on the base was imminent. The next day, an attack was launched by about 300 NVA troops and the base was under heavy shelling. The 304th PAVN Division arrived, and General Westmoreland formed "Operation Niagra," a U. S. 7th Air Force air support defense campaign. Enemy shelling quieted down until the last week in January to the first week in February.

We were there to assess the capabilities and feasibilities of launching Hatchet Force missions from there to hit enemy lines of communication in northern Laos. Khe Sanh had been under enemy attack since mid-Janaury. Many scholars felt that General Giap saw Khe Sanh as a possible, and highly viable, diversion from the impending TET offensive. The only overland supply route was virtually closed. Under air cover of A-4 Skyhawk fighters, the hilltop area received supplies from helicopters and the main base by C-130s. I was not too happy about this assignment. However, it was just another mission, and I would do the best I could while trying not to get killed, which might be difficult. Loading up to leave Da Nang, I was a little surprised when I spotted a West Point classmate, Mark Walsh, who was looking to hitch a ride to Khe Sanh. "Come on, buddy," I said, reaching for his hand, and he hopped aboard.

An elite SVN Army pilot deftly maneuvered the H-34 helicopter into the Khe Sanh base, the bird's rotors never stopping and grinding out their loud hums. It was a hot LZ (landing zone under fire), and tracers whizzed by. Our pilot seemed to pay no attention to the tracers, but adrenaline was running high and I am sure his hair was standing up on the back of his neck as it was on ours. He barely touched down before we were out and running toward the surrounding bunkers. The H-34 was gone. The pilot was so familiar with the terrain, he probably could have flown in and out with his eyes closed. We had about 10 seconds to make it to the safety of a bunker before we faced the possibility of getting our heads shot off. We hit the ground running. Safely in a bunker, Mark remarked, without a trace of humor, "Man could get killed around here." I do not know why, but this struck us as funny. We laughed until we nearly cried, and that seemed to release our anxiety. We were not there to fight, but we were lucky to be alive.

Completing our mission in three days, we were glad to leave, concluding that it would not be a good idea to launch from Khe Sanh. A couple of months later, one of the deadliest and bloodiest battles of the

Vietnam War in Khe Sanh was over. Estimates of dead enemy combatants range from 10,000 to 15,000 and up to 703 Americans and South Vietnamese soldiers. Obviously, there was a whole lot more that happened at Khe Sanh, a major Vietnam battleground, and much has been written about it. I did not participate in the Khe Sanh battles, but was only there for a short time. Khe Sanh was abandoned by the United States on July 5, 1968, and the NVA flag was raised. It was the first time that a major base was abandoned because of enemy pressure. General Giap declared victory.

8.

BATA BOOTS

Technically speaking, senior Vietnamese General Lam, was my superior. We were there to assist South Vietnam in the civil war, after all, and he was responsible for overseeing both the ARVN and the "White Mice," the semi-multi-national police force in Da Nang. I had heard from various sources that his modus operandi was of the worst kind, the financial type, a kind of shadow of Heller's "Milo Minderbinder," empowered only by his control of Da Nang's black market. Every dollar, piaster and piece of scrip introduced, inflated, or created by the war flowed through that market, be it aftershave lotion or kilo brick. The exception was arms, though I trust you could get an M-60 machine gun if you knew the right people. I was no economist, but I knew the American taxpayer underwrote every sou of this abhorrent baksheesh and I aimed to recover some of it somehow, some way, and I got my chance.

I hated General Lam, but not for any moral reason. I just hated him. We never met, but when our paths crossed, jeep-to-jeep on Quong Trung Street or the bazaar at the Con Market, I felt my animus telescoping like a rifle-sight, with him in the crosshairs. The NVA, his enemy, was my enemy, but even in war, it did not matter. Some people you just do not like and there is no way to understand it, particularly when you have not personally met them. While I respected the NVA as being among the best light infantry in the world, by July, I no longer felt beholden to whatever "rank" made this man my "senior," or answerable to the commercial and criminal code of the current pantomime of Da Nang's municipal government.

I had not realized the vastness of Da Nang's black market until I was there one morning in July 1968. Just back from a mission in Laos, I noticed a few of my Nungs walking kind of funny. "Bata boot," Mr. Huy explained. The Nungs wore sneaker-type boots of rubber and canvas that were good for the jungle because they dried out quickly, but had a shelf life of a pair of white-toed "All Star" Chuck Taylors. After my Laos mission debriefing at FOB-4, I made Bata boots my first priority. I visited the Supply Lieutenant, Tom Groppel. "Lieutenant," I said matter-of-factly, "I need 300 pairs of Bata boots for my Nungs."

"Well," he replied, "they are not exactly standard U.S. military wear. I do not even know if a requisition exists for them: local supplies for third-country combatants? Doubtful. In fact, I simply cannot requisition them."

"I am taking a Hatchet Force into mortal combat behind enemy lines, Lieutenant," I argued. "I do not think my Nungs should suffer, or perhaps lose their lives, because a certain piece of green paper does not exist. Would you not agree? Good God, can you not get them somehow? Can't you call someone?"

"Cannot do it," he answered, with so much

nonchalance, I came close to landing a punch on him in a very painful location. I might have had I been drinking, or not worried about getting into serious trouble, which I did not need. It would not have bothered me so much if that was the end of it: Bureaucracies impede progress, after all, and if a bureaucracy more obtuse than a military one exists, I have never heard of it. But my Nungs had no way of getting what they needed on the open market. They were reviled by our "allies," from the White Mice, who hounded them like Klansmen, to whatever merchant it would take to track down Bata Boots. That would probably take them to some factory in Cholon, the Chinese-immigrant section of Saigon, or back alley sweatshop in Dalat, the Central Highlands town from where many of my Nungs hailed. I had a very real situation on my hands, though not the kind found in a West Point officer training manual. It was a command decision, requiring the same time-honored resolution: Fix it yourself, or that failing, go up rank, which I did, without any satisfaction.

"Charlie, I honestly do not know what to do," said Lt. Colonel Overby, FOB-4's commander. "Nothing downtown?" I could see Bata boots were not on his priority list and as far as he was concerned, that was the end of the conversation.

Indeed, downtown was where the Bata boots turned up. "Daiwi," one of the Nungs said excitedly, as he entered my billet with a mug of coffee two days after our return from Laos. "I see beaucoup Bata boots on

Son Nuy Street. Con Market."

"Shit," I said. The black market was the last place I wanted to shop. But I was down there a half-hour later, just not alone. Lt. Bobby Blatherwick, two Nungs in front and two in back, piled out of the jeep into the bazaar. In the first rows of blankets, cheap card-tables and impromptu stalls, I fingered the merchandise, testing the waters: Marlboros, Kools and Luckies (doubtless pilfered off the docks in Saigon or Da Nang), Scotch, camouflage fatigues, canned food, so-called "fresh food." The place stank from an open sewer that ran through the middle of the street. Razors, transistor radios, batteries, standard-issue combat boots, cheap toys and cheaper watches, were the next block down, followed by an open-air livestock market another block down: goats and pigs; a couple of big oxen; fish, fish, and more fish. At the far end of that market, sure enough, was a street corner, Son Nuy Street, filled with Bata boots, the first street of the market's military section. The four little guys froze when they saw the boots, which was unlike my Nungs. These people kept their own counsel at all times, except when very drunk. I realized then just how torturous their boots must have been, but they did not complain. I raised my hand. "You be cool," I whispered. "Just be cool." Stepping out of the Jeep, I was aware that we were of insufficient force, not to mention of proper attire, to strike the best deal in this particular market. The Nungs' involuntary reactions on seeing the boots galvanized me. My Nungs coveted those boots. They needed them, and by God, they were going to have them. We just needed a second trip. These merchants were either going to see the light of day, or this was going to be a five-fingered bargain. They had someone behind them to whom they paid protection money. Whether or not it was General Lam, I do not know. I anticipated - indeed counted on - tough negotiations. I would have loved to shoot one or two just for the hell of it. I could plead self-defense and throw myself on the mercy of the court.

The Big Daiwi and the Little People were headed downtown for the second time that day. Lt. Blatherwick was not with us this time. No need for another highly trained American soldier in jungle fatigues, web-gear with grenades, magazines, black gloves, and SOG knives. I wore my Green Beret and had a full magazine in the Car-15. Twenty rounds at the slightest pressure would accomplish whatever I might need. *Brrrrpapp.*

This was the Nungs, going on mission, who liked the fluid, more soothing cadences of soul better than country rock, or Top 20, so we had the Specialist rather than the Chicken Man on as the soundtrack for our car trip. "This is Specialist Jerome T. Watson, Radio Da Nang, with a little Smokey Robinson today for your listening pleasure."

"Fi ho!" the Nungs screamed from the back of the deuce-and-a-half. They drove in front, and the second Jeep was behind the one I had requisitioned from Colonel Overby without his specific knowledge. No one would ever tell him about it and I conveniently reasoned there was no harm since it was being used it for a good cause "Kwah!" the others yelled back in unison. "Flying Tiger! Strong!" They kept the chant going all the way up from Marble Mountain. The whores outside the Dog Patch shanties flipped us the bird as we sped past. They hated the Nungs like everyone else here. It was good to get on the Song Hai Bridge, where the military police of C Company gave us rather puzzled nods from their elevated observation towers and the sandbagged pillboxes at each end, as did the sentries at each of the fourteen spans along its 1700-foot length. The Bridge was the great military artery of Da Nang, used not only by Special Forces and the 3rd Marine Amphibious Force across the river, but for a good many troop and material movements down the length of I Corps, where transit was always safer and easier near to water. But I doubt anyone on that bridge had seen a Hatchet Force come across at full-throttle mission-pitch and in battle dress.

We opened eyes on the other side of the river as well: women and children outside the private houses at high noon, the rag-trade types, out smoking by the stone walls of 18th-century merchant houses, decorated so colorfully with poems, symbols and patterns. The Con Market was south of downtown's honeycombed streets and back alleys, past a small cemetery of the old French garrison, the graves filled with soldiers who died not in battle but from disease. Microbes: colonialism's great weapon of mass destruction. From China Beach up, I took it all in, the incredibly dense history of the place, in a way I rarely did. Not Master of all I survey, as usual, as I was on shaky ground now, and emotion, to put it lightly, was running high.

This is a win-win situation, I told myself. *This is an important mission; I'm here for the boys. I'm recouping the American taxpayers' dollars.* But I kept hearing another voice too, the same words over and over: *Honor, duty, and country.* I had taken the law into my own hands here more than once, but this was the first time I could remember being sober.

Mr. Ki, the Sergeant Major and the Nungs' second in command, yelled "Fi Ho! "Kwah! Manh me!" We were pulling up to the bazaar. Mr. Huy and two privates went ahead with the vehicles to Son Nuy Street. The other two Nungs and I hit the pavement. This time I felt we had sufficient force for what we had come to do. It was lunchtime, and the place was relatively empty. Still, there was a scurry as everyone backed up as we passed, a few blankets disappearing ahead of us rather quickly. The reek of fish and garbage was nearly insufferable. The food here always smelled worse than when actually cooked and eaten. At the corner with the Bata boots were three men, two scrawny guys who probably ran the concession, squatting the way these people did to relax, and a paramilitary type, probably overseeing the military part of the bazaar. A dyed-in-the-wool Mafioso, maybe five nine, tall for the country. He wore a gold Rolex, bracelets on both wrists, and his mouth was filled with gold teeth. I could make out his bulbous eyes through his dark green sunglasses, and doubted he was military, despite the ARVN Airborne insignias he flew on his Vietnamese Ranger tiger-stripes. This was a criminal, not a fellow soldier, and I was sure the duds and brass signified nothing but this man's ego. These people, bedraggled as they might look, made their way through life on image.

"Where did you get the Bata boots?" I asked, wearing my best military face, trying not to show too much of the animosity I felt. The truck and two jeeps came around the corner, and Mr. Huy and the Privates got out, surrounding the three men. The man in the green sunglasses feigned "No Englee" until Mr. Ki started translating, which proved too much of an indignity for him. "Daiwi," he said, grimacing as he tugged hard on his filterless Ruby Queen, "Someone give them to me." That was the last straw. Looking at the mixed message of centuries of colonialism from my command jeep had me searching for the right-and-wrong of this situation. I had read too much Graham Greene to be the amoral tough-guy at such times. This thug had just lost on his own terms as far as I was concerned. He thought he was being smart: "Daiwi, I know who you are. Someone give them to me." Someone whom you cannot cross, I thought. If he wanted to go deaf and dumb, he had a right to the No Englee tactic. If he had stuck to it, well, maybe it would have been hard for me to stay hostile across a language barrier. But for him to come off it in a heartbeat? So he would not have to answer to a Nung? No. That was a crack in this tough-guy's armor: Racism was weakness and sensitivity, if those words could possibly apply, that he simply did not have the luxury to show me just then. This appearance-conscious Oriental man had lost some major face. "Well, you can give them to me now," I explained in my semi-official capacity: *Just a transfer of military goods from one source to another.* "These are beaucoup Ps," he said offhandedly.

"I do not think so." I pointed the CAR-15 at his heart, putting it at Full Auto. We had quickly moved to the more aggressive part of our dealing. All of a sudden I was in full mission mode, no longer thinking of anything but accomplishment and how 20 rounds would cut this fucker right in half. I was sure he was weighing the same thing, but no way was he going to show any emotion. I still do not know for sure if I would have shot the man. He did not show the slightest fear. Perhaps to his mind, dying at the hands of an American was acceptable. Maybe he had been a soldier once and young. Without turning to the Nungs behind me, I raised an arm: The sound of 17 M-16s locking and loading sounded musical at that moment. "They are going to Cock-a-dau you. Du Ma, Doo-Mommie." Mr. Huy had brought his M-60 with him, and at the sound of an M-60 bolt sliding back, the man looked over his shoulder. His eyes were bugging behind the sunglasses when he turned back. It is not easy to stare down the barrel of a shotgun, and he had not realized until then that he was surrounded. There is no feeling that induces panic more effectively. He swallowed deeply. Fear.

Enough for me. End of negotiation.

We gathered up every boot on the corner and put them into the deuce-and-a-half. Then we got to work on a few extras: camouflage blankets, because it got cold in the jungle at night, and every pair of fatigues we could find that were smaller than a 30-inch waist. Few of the Nungs could fill out the sizes that were available for their use at FOB-4. I had stepped over the edge, and I would have been happy to take over the entire bazaar, cigarettes and Scotch to aftershave lotion. As the Nungs' commanding officer, however, the man who had empowered them to regain more humanity than they had ever seen in this fucking country, it made no sense to squander it over a transistor radio. And if the White Mice were to arrive unexpectedly and find Nungs aloose, there would be fatalities that I would never be able to talk away or walk away from.

Colonel Daniel Schungel, who ran the 5th Special Forces C Company down the road from FOB-4, got the blame. He knew damn well who the culprit was, but what was he going to do: Order an inquest? Bring a black marketer to our side of the river to identify one of his own? No! Once the Big Daiwi and the Little People were west of the river, we were safe. Just a long afternoon of distributing Bata boots in the Nung's billet at FOB-4, an awards ceremony accompanied only by Messrs. Johnny Walker Red and Johnny Walker Black. The Nungs loved Scotch. What a ceremony it was. By nightfall, my Nungs and I had strengthened our already tight bond, the kind that saves lives, and holds lines under the heaviest fire. I knew I had not only violated the law, but also reinforced wartime's great law, which is implicit trust between officer and subordinate. My head was as high as I could hold it when I stumbled out of the Nungs' billet toward my waiting bed, across 200 feet of sand on the other side of FOB-4. However, a hundred steps later, I knew that bed was in the distant future. Colonel Overby's jeep was out. He would be downtown already, so I requisitioned the deuce-and-a-half for the second time. A truck that size is not ideal for drunk driving, but if for nothing else, I had to get the taste of Scotch out of my mouth. Only Jack Daniels could to it.   I never answered for the Bata Boots incident except for a large number of free shots that night at House 22. When word got out, I was a big Special Forces Daiwi, not associated with SOG.

One of the Nungs got married the next evening and the wedding party that started out with everyone having a great time, quickly went wrong. I would guess that the reason for this might have been the full tumbler of Scotch that was placed on every table of the 300-man wedding party. I had consumed one whole bottle and was blotto when White Mice confronted my Nungs who were shooting weapons at the wedding hall. Five White Mice were arrested. Later that night what sounded like a mini-Tet offensive broke out. The White Mice launched a company-size assault with light machine guns, M-79 grenade launchers, and CAR-15s on the police house to liberate their five fellows and, undoubtedly, in retaliation for the raid we conducted on the black market. Three White Mice were killed and from that time on my Nungs had to travel under armed guard everywhere outside FOB-4.

9.

22 LeLOI STREET, MACV/SOG
AND DEAD BUG

Our Safe House in Saigon, a beautiful 18th Century granite manse, was identified with two white characters **22** in royal blue ceramic tile affixed to the facade. A touch of the Boulevard St. Germain in the midst of third-world squalor, it was SOG's bar and occasional whorehouse. It was ringed with barbed wire, Jeeps, deuces-and-a-half, and a half-dozen Nungs holding CAR-15s out front, and a half-dozen machine-gun emplacements inside a few tons of sandbags. General wisdom was that it would take a battalion of the 82nd, and maybe two Marine battalions to crack the place. The irony of the address: 22, signifier of the paradoxical tautology of wartime, to coin an ugly phrase. LeLoi (the Law), even if Le Loi was an historical Vietnamese figure, a 15th century Emperor, which we pronounced Leeloy. Still, this irony sums up the import and atmosphere of House 22. By virtue of our training inclination, we were the law, the town pillars, and the Rotary Club of whatever Montagnard villages we lived in or had decimated. We had local wives, kids, and dozens - at times hundreds - of indigenous or semi-indigenous people at our command, looking to us for everything they needed for survival. Paradoxically, we were outlaws too, by fighting "illegal" wars in Laos and Cambodia, and at times, by acting in total disregard for civilian criminal codes that we called "moral." The secrecy and danger of our operations filled us with a dread that was equal parts boundlessness and constriction. Our heads were turned by an awareness of our superiority. In a very real way, we needed that extra morale. But there were late nights in House 22 when my ears would prick, listening to the ubermensch sentiments that advanced military training builds into the soul.

Down Le Loi from House 22 was the MACV Officers' Club, where we often played the drinking game, Dead Bug. We sat at a table on the second-floor with squirrel-cage windows meant to stop grenades from being thrown in, and stared at each other until someone screamed, "Dead Bug!" The last man to hit the floor, belly up, legs and arms pointing to the ceiling, bought the next round. It was a silly game, but it helped to release a whole lot of pent-up energy after a long day, and we were able to taunt the loser and imbibe free drinks at his expense.

I was on the MACV officers' club front steps with my buddy, Mad Mike, a SOG Lieutenant, one night after a two-hour Dead Bug game when a mechanized infantry Colonel took exception to our Green Berets. He said something that I do not remember, because two hours of Dead Bugging tended to erase details of just about everything, but it may have been something about glamour boys belonging elsewhere. I got it. It showed his envy of Green Berets, and I saw his look and that of his big Lieutenant, one of those adjuncts who think proximity to top brass gives them the same luster. Mike and I looked at each other. My eyes pointed left, saying I got the Colonel, and Mike nodded. We decked the two of them so hard their heads bounced off the brick stairway when they landed. They laid there nursing their heads as we ran off into the night. It was court-martial time, but not for us. We slithered down a drainage ditch beside the MACV on our elbows and knees, Ranger-style and E- and E'ed like sewer rats past the delicious charcoal odors coming from the Stone Elephant, the Navy's two-block fortress of a social club where the steaks were world-class, then past a few more darkened buildings down to House 22, where many rounds of Jack Daniels were bought for us. We were not toasting insubordination. That was the very last thing we would willingly countenance, for we understood the importance of the chain of command better than anyone. These were libations that we poured, and we drank to ourselves in sanctification. Whatever hell broke loose because of this would not reach us. Someone above would cover for Mad Mike and me tomorrow, because he had to, and that meant we were free tonight.

The doorway of House 22 was small enough to make a man stoop, especially if he happened to be six three, and goes in one abreast. I stopped, squeezed my shoulders through the doorway, and stepped into a deafening roar, an explosion of bonhomie and jovial approval unimaginable in peacetime. My Bata Boots escapade and my already well-known reputation had preceded me. I had been expected at House 22.

House 22 wasn't so much for entertainment as it was for our sanctification, which in our macho fashion, we needed more. This was particularly so when the sun went down. The night belonged to Charlie, but at the bottom of a bottle we could take back pieces, living out fantasies, harbored in safety and warmth at the moment. Pretty, funky girls, looking like people we had tried to kill that day, frequented House 22 in the well-lit downtown, west-of-the-river area. Sex was readily available, quick and hostile, strictly war-zone mentality, with absolutely no emotional entanglement. While I was no angel, I lacked the sadism to turn that into eros. In Da Nang, regular Army and Marines frequented the all-Asian whores in super-primitive roadside shanties stretched along the eastern highway past the Song Hai Bridge, in a place called Dog Patch, with earthen huts with roofs and siding made of crushed Schlitz and Diet-Rite Cola cans, and sometimes C-ration boxes. SOG always had the cream of the crop: Generals' daughters, German whores, or an occasional divorcee or socialite from someplace like Barbados.

House 22 wasn't just a party place, either. It was a court of highest resort, where debts got paid, or forgiven. It also served as a church, or in any case, the place where you did many of the things normally done in church. It was the only place in Vietnam, for example, where you would see SOG men with their heads down after a lost battle with the bottle, or giving way to the introspection or grief you could not afford out there, but which had to manifest eventually.

In the semi-darkness of House 22, Loretta Lynn shared the jukebox with Hoyt Axton and Merle Haggard. CIA gunslingers in green sunglasses and Hawaiian shirts stood two-deep at the bar, beside SEALS and once- and future- Hells Angels with Harley tattoos and T-shirts under tiger-stripes, Montagnard jewelry on every inch of their necks, wrists, and fingers and SOG knives dangling from their gun belts.

At House 22, guns had to be checked at the bar. There was to be no exceptions. Every night, the Sergeant-at-Arms sat there on a spectacular cache of weapons - CAR-15s, Swedish Ks, Uzis, and Brownings. Everyone felt equally bound by that particular law, and no one objected. However, being unbound was what House 22 was all about, and once in a while, the rule of checking guns wasn't followed, and someone got past the Sergeant-at-Arms.

My first night there, a Chinese Air America pilot with a pair of Thai hookers massaging his back, lost a mountain of piasters, dollars, scrip, baht, and a currency that I didn't recognize on a hand of some Oriental seven-card stud. Someone screamed when the hole cards were turned and his hookers began caterwauling when his opponent, a Vietnamese King Bee Cowboy, who flew H-39s for SOG teams, picked up his winnings. The pilot pulled a cannon of a gun from his jumpsuit and fired two rounds into his losing hand. It was probably a Colt, but it happened so quickly I couldn't be sure. I just remember when I looked around, I wondered whether to hit the deck or the Cowboy, and noticed that only a few patrons seemed to realize, or care, that a gun had just gone off.

A Recon Sergeant named Henry Salusniak pulled the pin on a grenade one night when he thought he didn't get fast enough service at the bar at FOB-4 in Da Nang. I was sitting with three Sergeants from II Corps, Virginia boys who were crying their hearts out when Merle Haggard came on the box, reminding them about the little women back home and about all the white-tails they had not shot in the time they were there. I saw the commotion at the bar first, then the grenade, and my training got me up and over there in a hurry.

Salusniak was a wiry mongoose in his 40s or early 50s, wearing sweaty jungle fatigues that had gone so long between washings they were pointing in creases that made no sense. A SOG legend, he was a former Czech soldier recruited by the OSS during WWII. He joined the 10th Special Forces as an A-Team Sergeant in the '50s and emerged in Vietnam as one of the Project's best recon Sergeants. His most recent heroic act was wire-tapping Ko Roc, an NVA stronghold west of Khe Sanh across the Laotian border. The intelligence he gleaned and gathered undoubtedly saved hundreds of Marines.

A Lt. from FOB-1 in Phu Bai was already pleading for sanity: "Drink, drink, drink! A bottle for the Sergeant! Henry, Henry, please. Henry. Put the fucking grenade away. Please! I'm buying. A bottle of John just for you and me. Eine flasche Johann, ya?"

His pleas went unheeded. "Henry can only trink by blowing place up! I in voods long time. I thirsty. I tired. I fed up. I fuck you where you breathe. And I no German!"

"Have a drink on me," the Lt. said. The Eurasian barkeep shoved him a bottle of Jack Daniel, and the Lt. filled a tumbler halfway and slid it to Salusniak, who drained it in one gulp. "Aaaah," he yelled, and turned to yell at the the barkeep. "You no see Henry? I too short? Maybe you too short, yes? I fuck you where you breathe." The glass was filled again.

Halfway to the Sergeant's post, I heard Henry scream again. It was just the recoil from shot #3, but it spun me back around. "Aaaah Capt., you good man. You make Henry happy. I have trink now. You have trink. I still fucking pissed. He held a grenade aloft. "If Henry vant trink, he get trink, yes?"

"Fuck you, Henry," a Triple Nickel pilot hollered from the other end of the bar to Salusniak. I had lost my bearings, and couldn't figure out what was the joke here, who was who, and if the situation was defused. I would learn later that the pilot, aglow in a Kelly-green party suit with shiny patches and zippers, was a top gun Migkiller in 555th Tactical Fighter Squadron Major "Fire Can Dan." I would also learn that these two fellows had a history. The 555th Tactical Fighter Squadron, out of Thailand, supported a lot of SOG missions. SOG, on more than one occasion, ran Bright Lights to save 555th pilots who had gone down. Two months back, Fire Can Dan had been hit above Hanoi.

Fifty-two mm flak had killed the co-pilot instantly, but Major McGraw got the Phantom over into Laos before bailing out, unfortunately into heavy NVA territory. He probably had 10 hours, maximum, before capture, but McGraw spent less than two hours in the jungle before Salusniak and a heavily armed Hatchet Force found him surrounded by an NVA company. Salusniak arrived on a Jolly Green CH-3 chopper loaded for bear with heavy equipment and mini-guns. He secured the Major, at the possible expense of being separated from the Jolly Green by heavy ground fire. Seeing that he'd never make it back to the helicopter, he had called for the big metallic bird and it arrived just in time, belching fire, pinning the NVA back into the jungle long enough for Salusniak, McGraw and the Hatchet Force to carve out sprinting distance from NVA firing range. The FAC called in an airstrike, but that left 20 minutes or more of run-and-gun before salvation would come from above. The North Vietnamese soldiers gained ground, knowing the jungle better, and time and again the Jolly Greens let loose with mini-guns, their terrible whining sounding like a million mosquitos. This provided enough protective fire to earn Salusniak and his men time to run or find better cover. A prop-driven plane with a lot of fire power, the Skyraider sortie, finally arrived. Salusniak popped colored smoke to let the FAC note his position. In that instant, the area behind him was engulfed in bright orange fire that only napalm can create. Most of the NVA company, the lucky ones, died instantly. Salusniak saw the few survivors, half-man, half-bacon, running like crazed dogs through the jungle, screaming in pain and trying in vain to rub off the burning jelly. The Major's extraction, against phenomenal odds, became one of the most documented war stories out of Laos: *The FAC upstairs in the O-2 Birddog watched it play out below him like a movie, Apache versus stagecoach, and narrated on a frequency many were tuned to back at C & C at FOB-4 in Da Nang.*

By ten o'clock that night, Salusniak and McGraw were arm-in-arm at the bar. I suspect Henry had his "trinks" brought to him that night, too. I am also sure that many such nights would follow.

Apparently, this night was not the first time Salusniak had pulled the grenade stunt: he just had this habit of showing you the pin whenever he thought service at House 22 was slipping. And, looking back, I realized that Fire Can Dan was able to use that grenade to finally "get out of the woods" with Salusniak the night I met the two. He may not have known it, but the bravery he showed served the purpose and Salusniak took proper note.

McGraw had heard of me somehow. His boss, Colonel Robin Olds, another former West Point football player, and American fighter pilot and officer, had seen me rush over, always the obedient cadet, when Henry pulled the pin. He had some choice words about the Air Force defeat of Army at Soldiers Field in Chicago, 1962, which I took in the same spirit he clearly meant it, and we were on our way toward being old pals. I reminded him, though, that we had whipped Roger Staubach in 1964. We were busy bonding when Salusniak rolled the grenade lazily down the bar in front of us. I didn't know what to think or do: Run? Duck? Once you gear up to smother a live grenade and stand down, the instinct to do it again isn't automatic. Fire Can Dan had his left hand around the entirety of my forearm at lightning speed, and the grenade in his right. He took a good look at it, then shook it in Salusniak's direction, as if to say "naughty boy," before throwing it in a 55- gallon drum set out for empties. "Extract that, you little fucking Commie." he said. Henry exploded with laughter.

I understand, now, that it was only then that the Major paid Henry in full for his extraction from the Laotian jungle, not with drinks, but with guts of his own. Henry put the pin back in the grenade when no one was looking, but Dan could not have known that when he picked it off the bar. Every other gunslinger, spook and officer in the place besides Dan and me were on the floor. I was only on my stool because I had been frozen down to instinct level by Salusniak's bizarre display. Dan was standing, I thought, because there was no doubt in his mind, or fear in his heart. In fact, he was picking up the check.

In Vietnam, you could always tell a SOG guy by the Rolex GMT Master on his wrist, by the way he stared you in the eye, strong and silent like Gary Cooper, when you talked to him, and by the way he had his head in the air. In Vietnam anyone who had been in the country within the last week walked with bowed head, like a dog on a walk, noticing every last little thing. You learned that watching a buddy lose a leg or his life to a mine. Not us: If we were not in places we should not be, Charlie's neck-of-the-woods - and he didn't mine himself - we had Montagnard point-men and Indochinese trackers eyeballing our paths before we would stumble or step foot onto them. In Da Nang, our trackers were Nungs. Farther south, it could be KKK, a splinter of the Khmer Rouge, recruited by the Company. Around Kontum, Montagnard warriors of the Rhade or Sedang tribes, or various other Yards walked point, ready to give up life and loyalty. The SOG bond with these people was strong. A lot of us were good 'ole country boys ourselves, and Vietnam was a place where a lot of old scores got settled and forgotten about over a few drinks. Dan McGraw would later fly me down to Bangkok, buy me the best dinner and worst case of clap a man ever got, then walk me through the lobby of the sybaritic four-star Continental Hotel in my jungle fatigues, web-gear, and packing my CAR-15, signing autographs and posing like a rock star for Polaroid Swinger pictures: "Are you really Special Forces!"

10.

THE LOST

"Fire Can" Dan McGraw, and I, led a team to Nakhon Phanom, Thailand, on a mission to rescue a SOG team that had gone missing across the Thai/Laotian border. Air cover was intense. We loved the Skyraiders A1E prop planes, which were equipped to carry more ordnance than the more oft-used jet planes and were capable of staying up longer than some others. Our weapons of choice on the ground were CAR-15s.

We put our team on the ground, and began a quiet and stealthy search, slicing our way through the jungle canopy. We dressed down, as if that would keep the enemy from knowing we were soldiers. There was some psychology, but we knew our enemy would not be fooled by our dress. Progress was slow, but steady, as we constantly listened for the sound of gunfire, a whisper, a voice, or other sign of the presence of enemy soldiers. There was nothing - not a hint that a human had ever been there. No bodies, no left-behind weapons, no military gear, or no water canteens. The team had vanished without a trace. Our search extended for a week, and we gave up the search because we knew, almost certainly, the team had been killed and disposed of in some unknown location, and our supplies had run low. Usually recovery efforts took less time.

During this period, I learned from various sources

about Laos' extra-military aspects. There were tales of opium trafficking, slave traders and ivory merchants to name but a few. I say this not because I think any of these things had anything to do with the team's disappearance. That will probably always, for me, be somewhat of a mystery, although, deep down, there is no mystery. To the best of my knowledge, neither the team nor the remains of its members have ever been found. In my quiet times, and more often than I would like, their faces creep in and I still see them as clearly as then. I suppose one day, somewhere, someone, not necessarily a soldier, will chance upon a pile of bones and not realize they have found the missing team of great soldiers who fought the good fight in Southeast Asia. They will not know that a team of highly trained searchers tried in vain to locate and rescue these men, or that someone still grieves for them.

The battalion of Nungs, which I had commanded in Vietnam, was lost about a year after I left, probably in 1969 or early 1970. I pay them the utmost homage. They fought valiantly and ferociously for a cause they probably did not understand, but they hated the NVA and did not mind killing them. I can only assume they were all killed by our mutual foes, but I always hold in my mind the thought that maybe, just maybe, some were fortunate enough to have assimilated into their own and survived, but my gut tells me otherwise.

Over the years, many teams went missing. Some were rescued, others not. If they were not found, there was really no mystery about what happened to them.

They either and been discovered, tortured and killed in unimaginable ways, placed into a POW camp, or quite possibly encountered planted ground weapons and been blown to pieces. Probably no one will ever know for sure, and their families still wait.

It was, I suppose, "luck of the draw" as to which teams returned intact. My unit and I were responsible for rescuing at least five lost teams. One found us first. We had been searching for several long hours, and nearly given up hope, but we kept trudging and chopping through the overgrown jungle, wiping away the sweat that trickled down our faces and into our eyes.

I remember that mission vividly. We flew directly out of FOB-4, which was unusual except in emergency situations. A recon team had been lost in the Tri-Border area, and I was to lead the Prairie Fire Recovery rescue mission. We were halfway through the triple-canopy jungle, going as fast as possible, working our way to where we thought they might be. We heard subdued voices and jungle sounds very close by and we took immediate cover. Certain we had stumbled upon a group of enemy soldiers, we laid chilly, hardly daring to breathe. Hearing footsteps and voices coming closer, we quietly raised our weapons and pulled out hand grenades, ready to wipe out a bunch of enemy combatants. What we saw was a bunch of tired, dirty, exhausted SOG recon men coming toward us, grinning through the grime. What a sight that was! Scurrying to safety, with the beloved Skyraiders' help, we evacuated under fire, with no loss of life. Later, we listened to the team leader's account of near capture and their escape. I was always gleaning, listening and learning. This mission internalized for me not only my advanced training, but also the prestige of SOGSF. I was enforcing my God-like persona. I was invincible!

11.

INTERCONNECTING FIELDS OF FIRE

I was a 26-year-old Captain into my eighth month in Vietnam, totally enthralled with both my role as a Hatchet Force Commander and my life in SOG. A Hatchet Force was comprised of Special Operations American and south Vietnamese members of MACV SOG. (Military Assistance Vietnam Special Observation Group). Our primary goals were to disrupt and destroy enemy lines of communication and supply, primarily along the Ho Chi Minh Trail. It was also our responsibility to rescue teams when they went missing in Vietnam, Cambodia or Laos. Hatchet Forces were relatively small, but the number varied according to circumstances. There was always a team leader, radioman and a medic, and at least three Special Forces men, and 20 to 40 Nungs. I am not certain why it was called "Hatchet" force. However, an extremely sharp hatchet can be a lethal weapon that we often needed, not just to cut through the jungle, but in close combat situations.

Unknown to me, I was about to lose some men under my command. The weight of my responsibility hit me full blast and sank in when Colonel Jack Warren, a very tough commander, briefed me on a mission that would take about 200 Nungs and me into the Song Cai River Valley in the heart of "Indian" country. My missions to this point had been successful, but the bloom was well off the rose. Death and moral turpitude surrounded me. In a few days, my entire life would be changed and I would never be the same.

"As you already know, this particular area is a great access route for the NVA. Your mission, as usual, Pfeifer, is to blockade and disrupt the enemy's lines of communications. It will be rough unless I miss my guess, but one I am confident you can handle. Keep your head up and your eyes open. There will be plenty of Arc Light activity, so that should diffuse the situation and move the bastards out of the valley, but don't count on it."

"I won't sir," I confidently replied, happy to hear that B-52 bombers would be working with us. They will wipe out the enemy there, I thought. I could not have been more wrong.

It had taken our Hatchet Force nearly three surreptitious days to reach the Song Cai River basin. We traveled in axis or parallel lines, 100 Nungs on each side of the River. I had tried, in vain, to suppress my fear and apprehension at being there in forbidden territory. To say otherwise would be highly misleading. I did not like the thought of even one of us getting killed or maimed. It was then, and still is, important to any commander that men are not lost on his watch. Becoming a prisoner was something we tried not to contemplate.

I had learned real freedom: Single file through triple canopy jungle, no borders, dog tag rank, taboo, or human laws. Mortal fear stole into my heart and had no effect except to galvanize me. In high alert mode, anxiety cut gut-deep and imbedded in my muscles. It was too late for anything except squaring my shoulders and assuming the bravado face that I had mastered. It was like I had snuck into a Rolling Stones' concert by the back door and security guards had not discovered me yet, but they knew I was there somewhere, and would find me soon. I had to be ready to run or fight. I may as well have walked in the front door. The enemy, should we confront them, would be fierce and unrelenting. The responsibility lay heavy to fulfill my mission successfully and protect my men.

The damn mosquitos were driving us all crazy. They seemed as determined to get us as the NVA. I hoped none of them were female of the Anopheles species, which caused malaria. I thumped my gear down and slathered repellent all over my exposed parts, wiping away the remains of several smashed mosquitos, which already had been sapping my blood. We arrived at our destination a few hours after an unsuccessful and massive B-52 Arc-Light strike intended to clear the area of NVA fighters, whose lines of communication we were there to interdict. Several acres of former mountain jungle had been reduced to a landscape resembling a Matthew Brady plate of Chancellorsville. The smell of cordite was overpowering. I could not imagine a B-52 Stratofortress strike being unsuccessful. They operated at altitudes too high to be seen or heard and carried bombs weighing from 500 to 2000 pounds. They hit enemy base camps, troop concentrations and supply lines in close air support situations and made advance operations as they had done here. First comes the sound of rolling thunder. Then, as the bombs strike the intended targets, the ground shakes and rolls like a massive earthquake, tearing up anything in their path. It is hell on earth.

"Get settled," I instructed the Nungs. "Keep your eyes and ears open." I realized I was repeating Colonel Warren's words to me. Some of the best light infantry in the world, the Nungs had great squad sense. Their very constitution and experience had taught them to be cautious, but it was my duty to remind them. In addition, they all carried CAR-15s, AK-47s and RPGs and were proficient in their use. I trusted their keen survival instincts. We quickly dug in with our mortars and waited, not really expecting a battle. It seemed we had reached the end of the earth and there was nothing to report. Eerily quiet, except for the jungle hum, I was surprised at finding no sign of enemy troops. Knowing the NVA as I did, I would have been greatly surprised not to encounter them at some point during this mission. I was right. The NVA had moved up river and somehow had managed to evade the B-52 attack. That night, around 300 NVA, a much larger number than anticipated, surrounded us and the fight was on. I had never been in a battle fought with more intensity.

I could throw the smooth-shaped M33 grenades 50 yards or more, like a baseball. Their serrated inside springs had a six-second charge time. I pulled the pins, let them cook off a couple of seconds and throw. They created pretty fine airbursts, with the ability to kill or demobilize a good number of the enemy. Ironically, the Vietnamese soldiers lacked the muscle strength and technique to throw well, maybe 20 or 30 yards. They had never played Little League. What did they know about throwing round weapons? They used cylinder-shaped stick grenades, or in British Army slang, potato mashers, like the Germans used in both world wars. Potato mashers had a 5-second timing mechanism. Unlike the fragmentation grenades, they were detonated by tugging a pull cord in the hollow cylinder.

Flares carved out enough light to allow us to scramble to the top of a ridge, amid fast and furious enemy mortar fire from across the river. The NVA men not only had the advantage of numbers, but of being able to see us better than we could see them. Unlike us, they could retreat at will.

We bunkered down in makeshift sandbag command posts between interconnecting fields of fire. The situation was critical, and I got in radio contact with the FAC: "This is Waterbird. This is Waterbird. Need help here now. Suggest you use anti-personnel (weapons primarily aimed at people). Your target is dug in across the river at the bottom of the ridge. Two or three hundred of them." Hot Shot Charley, Squadron Commander, was quick to respond. "Got you Waterbird. Comin' in for a look-see." The FAC flew in.

The enemy forces were on one side of the river and we were on the other. We fired our mortars, and

Spooky C-47 airplanes, carrying loads of small bombs and mini-guns, flew over the NVA side. At night, we dropped flares to illuminate the target area so Spooky could come back with their mini-guns and hammer the NVA. The NVA forces were so numerous, smart and ferocious, they kept coming back again and again for four very long days. We hammered them, and they hammered us with mortar fire and whatever weapons they could find. I could not afford to lose a man and I was in charge. What would the Nungs do without their Daiwi? I was their Captain, their leader, and they depended on me to protect them. A couple of Nungs started to leave their bunker and I hollered, "Get your asses back in before you get your heads shot off. Get back in!"

Suddenly, and unfortunately, an unbelievable barrage of monsoon-like rain began, making airstrikes impossible. I was utterly powerless. All I could do was wait. *God damn this war.*

I visited the piss tube, sat down and settled back. At the end of the second day, the water was up to my butt in that damn sandbag bunker. I waited for the monsoon to end. Suddenly, I heard the very welcome sound of an H-34 helicopter, the vehicle of choice in this type of situation because it had more torque than a Huey and consequently had an extremely quick "in" and "out" maneuverability. I was immediately on frequency. "Waterbird right below you. Waterbird here."

"I see you Waterbird. Bringin' you some grub and

water." The words were hardly out before I saw the helicopter begin to descend. Right in front of my eyes, it crashed and burned, and lay there on the muddy, slick hillside. For the next day and a half, the smell of burning magnesium hung heavy in the air, overwhelming even the rot of the jungle and the downpour. I was overwhelmed with helplessness, fury and, worst of all, uselessness. And I was so damned sad. It was like my divine right of being there was decomposing right in front of me and there was nothing I could do. I did not personally know the men on the doomed helicopter, but they were "brothers-in-arms" doing their share in this God-awful, and not known to me at the time, winless, war. I realized they were all dead. All I could do was order my men to remain hunkered in their bunkers, while the smell of the smoldering plane and its cargo overpowered all of us. I could not stop myself. I hated that helicopter, the men and the whole damn place in which I found myself. *Why the hell did you come in? Didn't you know you'd get killed or maimed? Now here you are, on this fuckin' mountainside with no way out.*

There, among the sandbags, in a foreign and forbidden land, I lowered my head, closed my eyes and pretended not see my fallen comrades, or feel the misery that surrounded me. The difference between here and Park Avenue was that here I was not among family that loved me, but among Nungs that may or may not love me, but tolerate me and even depend on me. I am surrounded by enemies, who do not necessarily hate me, but are, nonetheless, determined to kill me, and there has been a price on my head since my first mission. I owned Park Avenue. It was my safe refuge, not my temporary and dangerous, sandbag prison. Right then, I would have given all I owned to be back at Fort Benning, or even Bad Tolz, Germany, but most of all, with my family back home in our New York apartment. I let my subconscious wander back. Acknowledging the pretense, I gave myself over to the warmth of my mother's arms as she hummed familiar tunes. I heard her say as clear as when I was a boy, "Come on kids, we are going for a ride." I recalled my father's voice and that, somehow, soothed me as much as anything could, considering where I found myself. Now, if I could only "be bright, be brief, and be gone." Pulled back from my reminiscences by mortar fire much too loud and close to ignore, I ducked from instinct and habit. I wiped debris off my rear end, and settled back down to wait. Although difficult for me, I had learned patience that I lacked that at West Point, both in academics and football. I realized Army's victory over Navy had come only after prolonged patience and focus on detail.

The next day we remained at the mercy of the monsoon, relentless ordnance and sniper fire. Our intermittent return fire was ineffective and totally useless, but it gave us some semblance of hope of survival and of killing some of the bastards. It was touch and go. All the while, I mulled over how to outsmart the enemy, but found no answers. There seemed to be nothing to do but wait and hope the rain stopped soon. As quickly as it had begun, the rain ceased and I was finally able to call in essential airstrikes. The lead pilot of an F-4 attack came over the intercom: "Waterbird, Waterbird, this is Lazy Fox. Gonna come down for a look-see and want you to pop some smoke." I replied, "There's 300 of 'em southwest of our position." To the NVA, it must have seemed like fire from the bowels of hell when they took the brunt of it coming from the bellies of the whining F4 aircraft. Lazy Fox came in screaming. *Varoom! Varoom! Rap, Rap, Rap!* Planes, low to the ground, came back once, twice, three times, carrying hydrax bombs, that tore up bunkers and destroyed anything in their paths. After that cluster bombs killed any troops in the open, and were followed by Napalm, that burned and blistered humans, grass and trees alike. Everything. The final blow emanated from an electrically-fired, six-barrel, air-cooled, 20mm Vulcan Cannon, carrying a loud scream over a few seconds, and supported by plenty of machine-gun-like fire power. Even after all this, the NVA came back firing with a vengeance until finally nothing more was heard. Then we received a message from FAC telling us to be on high alert, as if we were not already. A much larger NVA force of about 400 or 500 NVA soldiers was moving in. The next day for about 10 hours, we hit the NVA's positions with unrelenting Close Air Support, aided by gas-burning, old-fashioned, magnesium H-34 helicopters. Finally, 15 Americans and 200 Nungs were safely evacuated out of the area. Surprisingly, we had suffered only minor injuries. I took shrapnel to my right thigh and have the scars to remind me.

After this, we loved the Air Force. They had neutralized a precarious situation and saved our bacon. The key to our success was mobility and the weapons we carried: throwaway tubes, CAR-15s, and grenades. The NVA carried AK-47s. In very close quarters we could dispatch a number of soldiers with a few well-aimed grenades.

This mission became a miniscule mark on my responsibility record, through no real fault on my part. On the way back into camp, one of the Nungs accidentally shot into the camp and killed a SOG man and two Nungs.

Some others and I were recommended for Silver Stars for "courage under fire" and being able to withstand the assault from the NVA for four days. For some reason I never learned, Silver Stars were never officially awarded.

A short time later, I was sent as liaison to Udorn Royal Thai Air Force base in Thailand, home of the Triple Nickel pilots of the 555th Tactical Fighter Squadron, to thank them for the great job their pilots had done in saving our asses at the end of those four days. We fought like hell to maintain our positions, but they are the ones that saved us. I walked into the Officers' Club wearing my jungle boots and my Green Beret, cocky as hell, just like them. A bunch of pilots, all American boys in flight suits, young and cool, with drinks in their hands, were leaning against the bar bantering back and forth. They looked me over before one of them asked, "Who the hell are you?"

"Chuck Pfeifer," I responded, with a quick and partially mock, salute. "I'm Waterbird." After introductions, slaps on the back and handshakes, we became acquainted. Although I did not need an explanation for being there, I offered one. "Just dropped by to introduce myself, express my appreciation for your help, say thanks, and buy you a drink," I explained.

From the far end of the bar, a young pilot rose from his seat and headed my way with a big grin on his young face as bright as the morning sun. "Waterbird!" he exclaimed, slapping me on the back. "I'm Lazy Fox. You are a fuckin' hero!"

"I'm an imposter," I said, feeling unusually humble. "You are the hero." He smiled, acknowledging the compliment. "Nothing like it, Captain. Pure exhilaration. Hell, I'm still not out of the clouds." I knew what he meant. "Glad to be of service," he added.

A couple of the guys planted their hands on their hips, stood back and looked me up and down in mock horror at how I was dressed.

"Couldn't you dress up a little?"

"Go to hell," I grinned, motioning to the bartender. "Drinks. Drinks for everybody!" I commanded. "Drinks all around. What are you havin' boys?"

I was honored to meet this group of heroic men,

who in all likelihood I would never see again except in my mind's eyes as they raced overhead. However, a bond was formed between the rescuers and the rescued that would not broken.

Back from Thailand, a Recon One Zero, my buddy, Lt. Mike Rollinson, and I decided to head out for a little R & R. Mike was about 6'3" and 210 pounds, with the look of invincibility. Muscular and all-around tough guy, he was fearless in the face of whatever enemy. He was also a little arrogant, but so was I, and that was okay and accepted. He also had a mean streak that I witnessed a few times, but we were good buddies, and had implicit trust in each other. I was happy he was on my side. My buddies and I usually hung out together on our trips to town, but this time we went our separate ways.

"Meet up here later," I called, starting up the street. I spotted a Huey Cobra pilot, obviously drunk, lying on the Officers' Club steps, his clothes bloody, wet and clinging to his body. The Cobra pilots escorted our guys into enemy territory and had undoubtedly saved more lives than anyone would ever know. I approached the Cobra pilot and asked, "Chief, what happened?" He looked up at me with bloodshot eyes and replied, "Bunch of Marines inside beat me up and pissed all over me." I helped the pilot to his feet, and got him cleaned up.

"Thank you Captain." He stuck out his hand.

"Thank you," I said. "Thank you." As I walked away, I called to him over my shoulder, "You stay cool, and good luck. Forget about this and don't worry about it. I will take care of the Marines." He managed a wide grin. He knew exactly what I intended to do. I thought about taking him with me, but I was headed to the Officers' Club. I entered the Officers' Club and walked up to a Marine Major, who had just ordered a drink. I got the bartender's attention, and showed him my palm. "Hold the drink. I have some business with the Major." The Major whirled to face me. "What can I help you with . . . Captain?"

"Major," I asked, "Are you the one who pissed on the Cobra pilot I just passed outside? I should kick your ass right now, right here."

"What the hell are you talking about?"

"I believe you know, but I just passed a wet and bloody Cobra pilot that you beat up. If you did not personally do it, you know who did, and that makes you responsible. What you did to that pilot was pathetic and wrong. The Marines always seem to need air support, and he could be the one who gives it and saves a lot of lives, including your lousy life. You think it's okay to rough him up and piss on him? That is totally inexcusable." I was glad Mike was not with me. I doubt that I could have restrained him from getting into a fight with a bunch of angry Marines, and I would have joined him. We might have wound up in a lot of trouble that we did not need, or get beat up ourselves. Marines are tough guys, so I tried not to mess with them unless I was drunk. Several officers' mouths were hanging open in surprise, and I would guess, maybe shame. One of the Lieutenants lifted the glassful of whatever he was drinking, and bit a hunk out of it as if to say, "I am tough too." I glared at the Lieutenant, "I hope you choke on it sonny." Staring him down, I abruptly turned on my heels and walked out.

Later, I met up with Mike and the One Zero. Totally drunk, we headed back to camp. Mike and I at any time, particularly when drunk, would fight with anyone. This time it was with a military advisor.

Lt. Colonel Daniel Schungel, who ran the 5th Special Forces (Airborne) C Company, down from FOB-4, had a huge dislike for our deportment, and with good reason. He assigned men to try to keep tabs on our escapades, which was not easy and kept them pretty busy. All our SOG men thought they were a bunch of pompous asses. We were always devising ways to keep them aggravated and occupied. Seemed they kept getting the blame and the pain for things we did and they had it out for us. We ran into some of Schungel's men and one of the Majors mouthed off to us. We then beat him up, along with a couple of others. We finally escaped through Todo Street in Da Nang to the club where there were Nung guards. We did not escape unscathed. We were both bruised and beaten too, but not as bad as that Major and his cohorts. When Colonel Jack Warren heard about the incident, he said, "Fuck it. Don't worry." We did not.

Jack Warren was not a big man in stature, maybe five ten, but he was tough as nails. It was rumored he drank a lot and sometimes got a little mean, but I never saw that. He was, very competent and took his responsibilities quite seriously. I found him to be a complex man, but I liked him a lot. My book would not be complete without a word about the friendship between Colonel Chargin' Charlie Beckwith and Colonel Jack Warren. As often as possible, Chargin' Charlie jumped in his jeep and headed down Highway 1 from Phu Bai to Da Nang to visit Warren. Chargin' Charlie was a big man, around six two or three, and a damned good and intelligent commander. He and Warren caught up, had a few drinks, watched TV, played cards and arm-wrestled. I happened to be at the Officers' Club one night when Colonel Warren and Chargin' Charlie were there. Warren introduced me to Colonel Beckwith. "Come over here, Captain," he said. "Sit down." He challenged me to an arm wrestling contest. This was one of his favorite things to do and most times he won.

"I don't think you want to arm wrestle me," I bragged, "I might beat you." That was all he needed to hear.

"Get over here," he growled. The contest was on. He was very strong, but I beat him. I never let him forget it. It was just one of many of our arm wrestling episodes. Being very competitive, he was damned determined to beat me and most times he did. I can still hear him laugh.

Beckwith had a long and brilliant military career. He suffered life-threatening injuries twice, once taking a 50-caliber bullet that injured his abdomen. He transformed the Florida phase of Ranger training into a more realistic and true Vietnam-oriented jungle setting. With international terrorism on the rise, Beckwith recognized as early as 1960 the need for a specialized hostage rescue, covert operations and reconnaissance unit. He briefed military and government officials without success for several years. It was not until the mid-70s that he was appointed to create Delta Force. During President Carter's administration, he was the ground force commander for the 1980 ill-fated mission, dubbed "Operation Eagle Claw," to rescue the American hostages being held by the Iranian government. Afterwards, Beckwith said: "...the mission was doomed by too much internal bickering among bureaucrats who did not have enough experience with high-risk missions."

Returning to Vietnam in 1968, he commanded the 2nd Battalion, 327 Infantry (Airborne) 1st Brigade, 101st Airborne, among many other command positions. He served in the Korean War, the Malayan Emergency and the Vietnam War and received the Distinguished Service Cross, Silver Star with Oak Leaf Cluster and Purple Heart. Colonel Beckwith died at age 65, much too young.

12.

HONOLULU

`My feelings of having mastered my craft were further reinforced when I took a five-day R & R trip to Honolulu, where my parents met me. We were invited to visit General Michael Davison, who was Commandant at West Point when I was a cadet there. He knew my reputation, remembered me well, and was impressed with my accomplishments after my dubious career at West Point. General Davison told me that his daughter, Mary, was in town. I called her. "Mary," I said, "you are in luck. I have tickets to see Jimi Hendrix. Would you like to go?" At the end of the concert, Hendrix played his infamous "Star Spangled Banner," and we both found the rendition somewhat offensive. We left early, ready for dinner and to enjoy the rest of the evening. However, that was not to be. As we exited the concert hall onto Honolulu Boulevard, a young man ran his motorcycle, full throttle, into the back of a truck, severing his right arm. Blood was running down the middle of the road. Pedestrians were watching aghast, but offering no assistance. Perhaps I was supposed to be at that time and place for just another day's work. We ran to him, both getting blood-soaked, and I stopped the man's bleeding. We waited for his transport to the hospital. Wanting to get Mary home before going to my hotel to change, we were still covered in blood when we arrived at General Davison's quarters, I could see the General's immediate concern and the questions in his eyes: "What the hell is this?" Then, "Oh, no, what has Chuck done now?"

"Captain Pfeifer," he said, after hearing our explanation, "I am so glad you were there to save that young man's life. I would say the timing was pretty good. That young man doesn't know how lucky he was."

General Davison invited my parents and me to his quarters for dinner the next evening, where we were introduced to the commanding general of the U.S Army of the Pacific. My parents could not have been more proud. Finally.

After my return to camp, I received a letter from the Mayor of Honolulu thanking and honoring me for my help. He did not mention the man's name, but I figured he must have been very important.

13.

VOICES OF THE DEAD

In early-August 1968, I awoke with my whole body sore and aching. With a 105-degree temperature, I was diagnosed with falciparum malaria and hospitalized. Numb and semi-paralyzed, barely able to move, and in unbelievable pain, I knew I was dying. Ten days later, I was still in the hospital, filled full of malaria-fighting medicines, all the while surrounded by death, amputation, disfigurement, and triage of the worst kind imaginable: missing limbs, missing faces and eyes. All day long helicopters brought in new casualties. At night, the C-141s took out the bodies.

When I was in the camp hospital, I received a surprise visit from Sean Flynn, son of actor Errol Flynn, whom I had met in St. Tropez during one of my summer European vacations when I was still in West Point. I heard that he was in St. Tropez, and knew that he and my brother knew each other from the The Lawrenceville School near Princeton, New Jersey, and I looked him up. I don't know how he learned I had malaria, but I was told that he had come looking for me when he was close by. He found the time to come see me, and we recalled our times in St. Tropez. I was pretty weak, but it was nice to see him again. Sean was under contract to "Time" and he traveled with Special Forces during the Vietnam War. He had briefly been a movie star, then went on to journalism. In 1970, he was captured by communist guerillas in Cambodia during the regime of the Khmer Rouge and never heard from again. A four-decade search ensued to find him and a fellow journalist, Dana Stone, and Sean was declared legally dead in 1984.

After I began feeling a little better, I was anxious to get out of the hospital and away from death and maimed soldiers. I pleaded with Colonel Jack Warren to take me back to full duty at FOB-4. Even though I was often unable to stand very long, he took pity on me and assigned me to a desk job. Although still weak, I had moved back into the tin roof hut, or hooch, that I called home. I was on track with clear sailing to Colonel's rank.

The evening of August 23, 1968, men passed the evening at FOB-4 and spent half the night playing cards and watching movies, as was usual. We were a little nervous because we had also been warned by a U. S. Marine duty officer from a nearby Marine facility that North Vietnamese Army troops might be close by.

Some men fell into an easy sleep, some not, but I was unable to sleep and still recovering from malaria. The heat was sweltering and I was desperately trying to get some rest as I listened to my roommates' snoring. Out of an abundance of caution because of the warnings, which I took seriously, I had ordered that CCN's night security patrol composed of a recon team, take along an M-60 machine gun when they climbed up Marble Mountain close by. Early in the morning, still on Marble Mountain, the team leader, One-Zero, destroyed an NVA mortar team below just as it was about to quick-fire its weapons.

Platoon Leader Geoffrey Fullen, First Lt. Robert Blatherwick and First Lt. Ronald Crabbe, returned from a mission southwest of our compound. Their orders were to make enemy contact and, if necessary, confront them with back-up from local Marine units. They had received unconfirmed intelligence of a large NVA build-up, and the mission had been aborted. Fullen told me that right after his debriefing, he said to Captain Williams. "Sir, there could be some real deep shit out there. How good do you think this information is? Should we be implementing some extra precautions?"

Capt. Williams replied, looking into his face, and then at the ground. "Maybe you better say a prayer."

I was aware of the NVA's possible presence, but I was not worried as the camp perimeter was well fortified. At 0200, the camp seemed quiet and safe. I was wrong about the safe part. The sky seemed to be a little more illuminated than usual that evening, but was ignored. The Marines often conducted Harassment and Interdiction operations late into the evening.

Suddenly, I was awakened by screaming and the wheezing *pop-pop-pop, pop-pop-pop* of many AK-47s, and the *rap-rap-rap* of CAR-15s, followed by *whomp, whomp, whomp* of mortar fire from the Nungs' billet at the extreme Southeast corner of the compound I thought it was probably a relapse of malaria and maybe I was dreaming. I mistook all the firing for what I called "fuckin' night firing" and that maybe the Marines had mistakenly put some mortar rounds into our compound. *Varoom. Varoom.* I quickly knew this was no dream. "Jesus Christ, " I yelled, "the Marines are fucking up."

About 100 of NVN's Special Operations Brigade had braved the waves of the sea clothed in camouflage scarves, loincloths, khaki shorts, or nothing at all, their bodies greased so as to slide or climb through, over, or under, the well-fortified perimeter of the camp, carrying AK-47s, grenades, RPGs, and five pound demolition charges carried in woven baskets. They knew our strength and that we would fight to the death, but they were well trained and ferocious. Dying did not seem to be a concern of theirs. Obviously, they were well aware they would be killed. I am sure they were surprised at their success, but I will never know. At first, I could not understand how they managed to get so far into the camp, having to bypass the perimeter's natural terrain and fortifications. Once in, their sappers laid silent and still and waited for a signal from the spy who had infiltrated, and the sound of their mortar attack.

The windows of my hooch were screened and the back and front doors were swinging plywood, hardly built to withstand an attack. I always slept with my Browning 9mm under my pillow. When the firing intensified, which still seemed mostly in the Nung section of the camp, I jumped up, simultaneously grabbing my weapon, and peered through my window screen. A mass of humanity was running through the camp. Suddenly, I found myself face to face with a sapper ready to blow a satchel charge. I quickly dispatched him, shooting him through the head, and he fell without a sound. I saw enemy combatants running toward my totally exposed Nungs. The dead guy's buddies let loose with their AKs through the front door of my hooch, but missed my roommates, and I screamed to anyone who could hear me, "Get under the bed! Get under the bed!" All the while, I was firing through the front door, trying to keep from being overrun and killed. My Lieutenant's hooch was right off the back door. It was open and a sapper threw in a grenade.

Clump! Clump! Clump.

The hand grenade rolled.

. Clump! Clump! Clump!

I grabbed my mattress and pulled it around myself before the hand grenade exploded and blew me out the front door onto the sand knocking me unconscious. I could not hear a thing, and waited until my head cleared a bit. Then I went in and jerked on my trousers and boots. I was lucky to find my web gear, its pouches already filled with most of the ammo I needed. I added a bunch of those lethal olive drab and yellow 33 fragmentation hand grenades designed for close combat. I had my M16 at the ready as I stepped out the door. It was hide and seek, search and kill. I hooked up with Sergeant Major Jim Moore and another of our unit and we began to search the camp. I went into the Hatchet Forces' hooch that had been nearly destroyed. I could not see anything, and almost fell when I stepped on Geoffrey Fullen's leg as he was trying to protect Travis Mills, who was yelling, "I've been gut shot! I've been gut shot." Travis was bleeding profusely. Geoffrey was a hero. Hands over his head, he threw himself over Travis' body to protect him from a grenade that had landed between Mills' and another soldier. Luckily, the grenade was a dud and did not explode, but Geoffrey fully expected to be blown to pieces.

"My fuckin' rifle will not work!" I screamed over the chaos, slamming it to the floor. Geoffrey pitched me Travis' CAR-15. He was not going to need it. Nearly dead, Travis still yelled warnings not to go out into the open, yelling that the sapper who had shot him was watching and waiting to shoot anyone who showed himself. Blatherwick managed to pull Travis back into what was left of the room. Blatherwick, another hero, went to work transporting as many wounded as possible to the base infirmary for emergency treatment.

Geoffrey's hand was shot and badly injured. He lay bleeding on the floor amidst a blanket of thumbtacks, which had fallen off a shelf. My Lieutenant had been hit and part of his ear was blown off and he was screaming and hollering. I grabbed a towel and bandaged him up. "You are okay. Just stay right here. Just sit there. You will be okay." He finally quieted and his bleeding stopped. "You stay here," I repeated, "just stay right here." What else could he do?

The pitch-dark camp had quickly become a battle zone. No one knew who to shoot or not to shoot, or even where to shoot. The enemy was dressed just like us, if they were dressed at all. Full-out chaos reigned, but miraculously, no one shot any friendlies. The NVA commandos sprayed ammo at anything in their path that moved. The smell of gunfire hung in the air like a metallic blast. One of our men had his finger shot off while successfully killing his attacker.

I was in the mood to kill as many of the bastards as I could, especially after I came across a very good friend, Rolf Rickman, lying on the sand as I moved through the camp. I bent over him. He was gone, probably killed instantly. I became a mad man, mad as hell, filled with adrenaline and blind rage. Those fuckin' bastards are gone. Gone to hell with their 5-pound charges and their stupid baskets. I killed over a dozen of them and I loved it. I helped lead the counterattack that ran the bastard commandos out of the camp, but not before they had inflicted untold misery upon our brave soldiers, our equipment, our helicopters and, indeed, upon our psyches. Before the fighting ended, 17 American Special Forces men, 40 Nungs and nearly all the enemy Vietnamese commandos were dead or badly injured. Down below, the fighting was fierce and our telephone and radio communications center was knocked out with high explosive charges. Three brave soldiers died on the spot from the high explosive charges. Almost simultaneously, gunfire and explosives killed at least five Sergeants First Class.

Some Green Berets dashed and made it to a mortar pit and fired illumination. The NVA sappers took cover, lying low under walls and buildings. We waited for them to stick up a head or come out of the shadows. Then we shot them dead and retreated quickly. As the Sergeant, a Spec 4, and I made our way through the camp and approached the Mess hall, we saw a Sgt. Major and other bodies strewn around. We could not tell in the darkness who they were, and we did not have time to find out. On the way, I killed two enemy soldiers with my CAR-15 and moved on to the rear of the mess hall, where we found some teammates. A bunch of NVA, 15 or so, had dug in and were hiding around our Tactical Operations Center, but they would not be there for long.

Then I saw the craziest thing: One young enlisted man pulled a John Wayne. He moved toward the TOC in a fully exposed open area. I could not hear his words, but he waved his arms to gain the attention of the commandos, and tried to talk them into surrendering. He was instantly shot and killed. I could not comprehend why he did this, but in the heat of battle sometimes sanity and reason disappear. He apparently had not yet learned that the enemy would always choose death over surrender, and he paid for it with his life.

We are dug in North of the Mess Hall. "Boys," I yelled, "Give me some more hand grenades." I got about eight or nine. One by one, I pulled each grenade's pin, let it cook a couple seconds from its six-second-charge time and threw it. We got enough air bursts to see our enemy and killed all but three of them, who now fled in the dark with their names on a lot of bullets. They scattered throughout the camp. The TOC was on fire and we were still nestled in and around sand bags. We found and killed one of the commandos, and looked for the other two. No way in hell would they escape. Finally able to extinguish the TOC fire, we entered the main building, where we found Colonel Warren and Colonel Cavanaugh from Saigon who had come in for debriefing and to assess the situation. Tables and desks were overturned, and I yelled to them that the TOC had been secured. Colonel Warren and some other men left the building with me. It was around 5:00 or 5:30 or so and getting light. With our guns at the ready, we walked around the camp perimeter, gathering our bearings and regaining our wits.

Soldiers emerged from every direction trying to recount and understand what had happened. We were in shock, disbelief and barely holding onto sanity as we assessed injuries and fatalities. We were still looking for the two missing commandos, but I knew we would find them soon and I wanted to be the one who made sure they were killed. I was looking forward to it. I had a taste for killing them now, and two more dead NVA commandos would be just fine with me. The camp was a mess and there were dead Nungs and Green Berets everywhere. Without a second thought, I put more bullets in every enemy combatant I encountered, even though they were already dead. Later, Colonel Stephen Cavanaugh and a bunch of us were in the camp bar, where one of our enlisted men gave the Colonel and me much-needed drinks. One of the Nungs burst in, yelling "Daiwi! Daiwi! We see in shithouse, we see in shithouse!" and pointed to the latrine. I grabbed my CAR, checked the magazine, strode out to the shithouse and riddled it with bullets. Inside, a grenade exploded. The two escapees blew themselves up and the whole building flew apart, spewing pieces of it in every direction. The concussion knocked the breath out of me. I landed on the ground. It was surreal and primal and it terrified me. One commando died instantly. The other was barely alive and lay gurgling until I finished him off.

During the fighting, Bob Blatherwick, under fire, jumped in a jeep and shuttled the wounded to the camp hospital. He saved a lot of lives that night. When things had settled and we saw the jeep, it was riddled with bullets, but he never took a personal hit.

Jack Warren ordered us to the headquarters in Da Nang where General Cushman debriefed us. The night had been one that no one could have imagined. All my physical and mental energy was expended, not only from the fight, but also from the after-effects of malaria. I had been knocked nearly senseless and took some shrapnel to my left arm, but I was alive.

Bruised, rattled, angry, disoriented and emotionally wasted, I wanted to scream in anger at those sons-of-bitches commandos, dead or alive. I wanted to wail in despair, but tears would not come. I fell asleep in my billet out of sheer exhaustion and awoke with a terrible ringing in my ears and a throbbing headache. Soon, I would learn that 17 Green Berets had perished, the most in a single incident in the history of Special Forces. The battle lasted only hours, but the effects will last forever. I was lucky to survive the carnage.

I would probably be 99% correct in saying that the NVA singled out FOB-4 for attack because of its continued success in killing and maiming their commandos and in interdicting their crucial lines of communications and supply lines along the Ho Chi Minh Trail. We had become their very worst nightmare It has been reported that the attack had most likely been in the planning stages for nearly a year and had coincided, whether by chance or intelligence, with increased activities at FOB-4. At that particular time, over 100 Green Berets were there to appear before a promotion board and all six FOB commanders had attended a SOG staff meeting there the day before. In addition, the SOG Command and Control staff stationed near Da Nang Air Base had been moved into FOB-4 and operated out of the Facilities office.

Supposedly, a day before the attack, "ZULU" (flash messages) and "TTY" (Secure Teletype) warnings were sent by the NSA to FOB-4's communication center, reading "ATTACK IMMINENT." Colonel Warren reportedly dismissed them as unreliable. He had implicit trust in the Marines 3rd Trac Unit to counter any insurgency attempt. The Major in charge wrongly felt that the villagers south of Marble Mountain were friendly to the U S. He mistakenly felt that enemy commandos could not evade the Marines. I personally have no way of knowing if any of this is true, but I would not discount the word of any soldier who believes it to be true. It would take a very long time for the full story of this battle to be told, and everyone has his own story. Other stories may be different from mine, but I know I never want to experience anything like it ever again. The problem is, I do. In unexpected places and unexpected times, it all comes back with a vengeance nearly as real as then, just as inexplicable and just as hard to understand.

In "Secret Commandos," John Plaster, a fellow SOG veteran, recounted that horrific night and cited the role I was fortunate enough to play. He credits my "phenomenal grenade throwing for saving many lives." I did all I could not only to save lives, but also to kill as many of the enemy as possible. I killed more than a dozen of them, and wish it could have been more. Some of us were immediately awarded Bronze Stars and later Silver Stars for valor. My Silver Star was presented to me at my Alma Mater, West Point. I wish Dean Dickerson and the housemother from Smith could have been there. I would have saluted them, properly this time.

14.

GOODBYE VIETNAM

A few days after the August 23, 1968, FOB-4 battle, I awoke feeling very weak with a high fever. My malaria had returned. The last day of August 1968, I was choppered out of FOB-4. It was then I was told about the sad fate of my good friend, Sergeant Rufus Rawlings, that good ole' Kentucky boy, who kept his Winchester 97 pump shotgun on the wall, hammer at full cock and loaded with double-aught buck, just like he would do at home. To me he seemed invincible, but I learned that during a mortar attack on Thong Duc, his shotgun fell over and discharged, killing him instantly.

I knew killing was what war was about. I just never knew it would feel so bad, take such a toll, or feel quite this personal. It was visceral and raw, and reached into and embedded into my inner core. It was the enemy or me and there was no room for hesitation. In 1968, I would blow off his head before he got a good chance to blow mine off. It became that simple.

I spent about a month and a half in the camp hospital in Da Nang, before being transferred to an Army hospital in Yokohoma, Japan, where I credit a great Navy doctor for saving my life. He knew just what to do. He filled me full of Primaquine and Chloroquine. In mid-November, 1968, I was off to Tokyo for more treatment. I was honored that General Michael Davison, my West Point commandant, whom I had visited in Honolulu, came to see me. I flew back to the States a week before Christmas 1968, and entered St. Albans Hospital in Queens, New York, and remained hospitalized there until fully recovered, which took a long six-month period.

My time in Vietnam was over. I did not do a short stick countdown of my last two months. Men actually take a stick, chop off a small piece for every day they have left to serve, and wind up with a small piece – a stump - to keep for a souvenir. I had reached the pinnacle, and the end, of my Vietnam experience. My last missions in Laos were the culmination of seven years of training and now nearly nine months of combat. I enjoyed and appreciated the superior training. However, I had come to the end of possible accomplishments: the missing SOG teams, the withdrawal from a promising opportunity farther up the Song Cai, the possibility of a higher rank and who knows what else? This river, the Song Cai, home to all types of activity, had become my personal metric, my measure of successes and failures of my excursions into enemy territory. It had also had tested the limits of my endurance.

Quite a few of my teammates and I needed to finish our tours, and we wound up together at Fort Devens, Massachusetts, named after Civil War general Charles Devens. It was the home of the 10th Special Forces Group (Airborne) from 1968 until 1995, when the Group moved to Colorado. I worked in the Operations Center there until my tour of duty was finished in June 1969. Daiwi's war was over not because of bullets, Napalm, grenades, Toe Poppers, Potato Mashers, or Vietnamese commandos. Daiwi had been conquered - done in by a small, night-biting female mosquito of the Anopheles species. It would be all mental now, but would manifest in the physical as well. Leave it to a female to do the job. Waterbird down.

15.

ADVERTISING AND INTERVIEWS

After my discharge from the military in 1969, I cast around New York for a while, getting back and acclimating to civilian life. What the hell do I do now? I looked up old friends and tried to settle. My stepmother knew many high-ranking advertising executives all over the world, and she contacted Joe Standart, Senior Vice President and Management Supervisor at Young & Rubicam. I was hired as Junior Assistant Account Executive, and placed into the Goodyear Account group. I could have worked on Wall Street, but had no desire to do that, as it didn't offer enough glamour. I settled in at Young & Rubicam and learned how the advertising business, domestic and international, worked. I appreciated the outgoing and door-opening aspects of the business. The great Edward Ney, CEO of Young & Rubicam, a much-loved and respected man, took me under his wing. An imposing figure, he walked the halls stopping to chat, asking questions and making casual observations. Years later I interviewed him for "Quest Magazine." When he died, I was asked to deliver a eulogy at his funeral. I was greatly honored to do so.

Malcolm Buddy Kahn, of Wilde Films, shot quite a few of Y & R's commercials. The first time I met him we talked a few minutes. I was impressed with his knowledge. He rather surreptitiously pulled me aside.

"My boy," he said, clutching my arm, "come and see me next week. I want to have a talk with you."

"Okay," I replied, wondering why in the hell someone as big in the business as Buddy Kahn would want to talk to me. I was more than a little dubious, but I could not control my curiosity. I went to see him. "I'd like you to be part of my company," he said. "I think you could sell dog shit off the sidewalk." That is how I became a director's representative for Wilde Films.

I promoted ad campaigns for Kahn, and I met a lot of people in the business, including Eddie Bianchi, who came to work for Rick Levine and me at Rick Levine Productions. Eddie suggested I might be a good candidate for a Winston Cigarette Ad campaign, which was in the casting phase. "The man lucky enough to snag this gig is going to make a lot of money and become a big star," he told me. That turned out to be true. Another actor/model was under consideration, and at the last minute, my name was tossed in. I was not confident about getting the job. All the "big dogs" were involved in the ultimate decision, and they had to be sure that the fulcrum for their cigarette advertising had the right look. I did. Inadvertently, and totally by chance, I became one of New York's biggest male models. A life-sized picture of me towered over Times Square. It was on the back cover of "Time Magazine," on the glossy pages of almost every magazine in the city, on the sides of city buses, and on billboards all across the world. I was Winston's urban and sophisticated counterpart of the more rugged, cowboy image of the Marlboro Man. Smoking was socially accepted then and few considered it harmful. My image soared. Joe Hunter of Ford Models signed me and I went on to do a lot of modeling work, including a Seagram's ad campaign, and modeling clothing lines for the photographer and clothing designer, Karl Lagerfeld, and other designers.

Oliver Stone became aware of me and cast me in the first "Wall Street" movie in 1987. Because of the publicity I garnered, I continued to get offers for movie roles, and talk show gigs. I became acquainted with Dana Carvey, John Belushi and Jon Lovitz of "Saturday Night Live" when my production crew shot some of their episodes. In retrospect, I believe this is where I met and became friends with the somewhat elusive Christopher Walken, but I'm not sure. It could very well have been at Elaine's iconic restaurant. Elaine had been a good friend of my father and now was my friend. My buddies and I got away with a lot more with her than did most customers. If she didn't like you, you didn't get in, or if you got in by mistake, she would see that you got thrown out.

I became one Manhattan's hottest commodities, and the subject of many magazine articles. Ivan Solotaroff wrote an article for "Esquire," titled "Ballad of the Green Beret," Chris Meigher of "Quest Magazine" did an article titled "Farewell to Arms," and "WWD" did a piece on me and my then wife, called "The Quality People." Spencer Morgan wrote "The Wild Purple Heart of Chuck Pfeifer" for the

"Observer."

I conducted interviews with Norman Mailer, Angelica Houston, Christopher Walken, James Woods, Bruce Cutler, one of John Gotti's lawyers, who would not do the interview unless his lawyer, Eddie Hayes, was present, Oliver Stone, and one of the most powerful men in the world at the time, John Lehman, the 65th Secretary of the Navy, appointed by President Reagan in 1981. Interviewing Lehman was somewhat like interviewing an emperor. He had a lot of assistants, mostly Admirals. It was very official. I have to admit I was a bit nervous, but it turned out to be a really good piece and well received.

One of my best interviews was of Norman Mailer. He frequented Elaine's. When we were introduced, he looked me over and remarked, "You look like a fuckin' Irish gangster." After many nights at Elaine's and other clubs, and after many boisterous verbal exchanges, we became great friends. If I had had to choose a father other than my own, it would have been Norman Mailer. A brilliant writer, he was tough, boisterous and fiercely loyal. He lived life to the absolute fullest, had a great sense of humor and a very low threshold for stupidity. He often said, "Chuck, you know over 51% of the American population is stupid," and he meant it. He loved to hang out, drink and raise hell, and I loved the man. He was a great listener and giver of advice. If he did not like someone, they knew it, but he was generous with his time and talent. Norman was human. He quoted once, "I've made an ass of myself so many times I often wonder if I am one." He was a man that made one think he would be around forever. I am proud to have known him and to have a number of his written works.

My wife, Lisa, and I briefly met General David Petraeus when we flew to South Carolina to attend one of his speeches at The Citadel. Our picture with him there appears herein. I subsequently interviewed him for "Quest Magazine," which was a little like the interview with John Lehman so many years before - controlled and military-style. I had expected that, but over lunch, he was very gracious with his time and in answering my questions. Lisa had the privilege of shooting his pictures for the article and she considered that a great honor. Most recently, I interviewed actor Harvey Keitel for "Quest Magazine," simply titled "HARVEY."

When I made plans to go Vietnam in 1993, I told my friends that I intended to interview General Giap. All they said, after rolling their eyes skyward, was "Yeah right, Chuck."

This was most notable interview of my career. I had not allowed myself to really believe he would grant me an interview. The great General Vo Nguyen Giap, who led North Vietnam's army in the French Indochina War and during the Vietnam War, was probably not going to do that. Although he was aware of my past interviewing successes with major figures, I had almost given up hope. The next to the last day of my trip, about 10:00 in the morning, I received a call from his headquarters. There was no preamble. Just, "General Giap will see you now." With no prior warning, I had already had a couple of Jack Daniels. He made me wait until the last minute, probably deliberately. He was not my friend, nor I his, but I was not there as a soldier, but more as a diplomat/reporter. I certainly was not his counterpart. That honor would have gone to several dozen others, particularly to General Westmoreland. I partially credit my first minder, Nguyen, for helping me get the interview. Although I am quite certain she did not particularly like me, she respected me, and put in a good word. It also helped that I was very polite to the General's press secretary and to some of my former enemies.

I was both elated and awestruck, and more than a little nervous as I entered General Giap's office. I saluted him, wondering if he could smell the Jack Daniels in my sweat. It was a little awkward - just a momentary silence - but it hung heavy. I realized he was waiting for me to speak. He motioned Paige, who had accompanied me with our equipment, to sit. One of his men quickly responded and held her chair. I waited for the General to sit and I followed. "I imagine you know me already General," I began. "Thank you for meeting with me. It is a great honor."

His smile was benign, but friendly. "You are well known to me," he countered. "Quite well known. Your call name was Waterbird. You were a MACV/SOG Captain, headquartered at FOB-4." I detected a long-past remembrance in his half-smile.

I knew, as he did, that the whole damn war was still fresh in both our minds. "And," he continued, "a fearless and formidable combatant. Oh yes, I know you well." There was that smile again. He knew everything about me. I would have been surprised if he had not. I figured he was the one who placed a price on so many heads and wondered who the bastards were who would have collected the money. I was wrong. The General turned and motioned one of the men to approach us. "Meet the officer who placed the price on your head," he said. "But, you know, of course, there was a price on the head of every Green Beret and many others. He commanded the raid on FOB-4 that you, undoubtedly, will never forget. But right or wrong, that is over now, don't you agree?" I was dumbstruck, but I believe I concealed it well. The officer was about five eight and maybe 55 or 56, with few wrinkles, even in the corners of his eyes. I found it difficult to guess the ages of Vietnamese people, whose faces seemed to stay perpetually young. The commander and I nodded to each other in mutual respect as soldiers, but nothing else. His eyes were cold and seemingly uninterested, although I doubted that. My anger was refreshed for the man to whom I had just been introduced. General Giap was quick to pick up the coldness that the commando and I felt for each other and he quickly changed the atmosphere and began to give me the "Party" line.

I removed the combat parka I received while training with the British 22nd SAS Commando Team in Bad Tolz. "I would like you to have this as a gift," I said to the General, holding it toward him. He refused it at first, then took it with blithe indifference, and smiled at Paige, as if to say, "For your sake, I will." As the interview moved along, however, he became friendly, kind and gracious, and I discovered he had a good sense of humor. I respected his obvious brilliance and his dedication and allegiance to his causes and country and could understand why he was referred to as the "Red Napoleon." He was short in stature, but I am confident this was not the reason he was called Napoleon. For many years, he had been instrumental in changing, or attempting to change, the political make-up of Vietnam. He planned the TET offensive. He had been as ruthless, cunning and devious in his country's causes, as we had been for ours.

It was an old military leader and politician, who had done all he could to further his own and his country's ambitions and goals, and one enemy combatant, who had done the same. We had both reached the end and acknowledged the result. However, General Giap lived for many more years, and I would imagine never quit commanding, just as I have never quit remembering or reliving the whole Vietnam experience.

It was a "People's" war, he said, in what I thought to be a rather wistful tone. I agreed, in more ways than one, although our individual interpretations would be a lot different. Ours had not been a people's war, but a personal one, just as his had been. It is not the people, but a lone soldier who loses limbs, eyesight, and suffers mental disabilities. It is the lone soldier who makes the ultimate sacrifice. The people are only peripherally affected. Children lose brothers, sisters, mothers and fathers. Wives lose husbands, and husbands lose wives. Parents lose children. Soldiers are sent to fight at the will of their leaders. Only ostensibly, is it for, or about, the people. Wars are politically motivated and politically fought, so perhaps, after all, all wars are people's wars.

As we left General Giap's office, the commando I had just met walked out with us. Without a beat, he looked at me and said, "I do not like you very much."

"I do not like you either," I replied, smiling. He politely nodded to me and walked away, but he was not smiling. Too bad I did not have my CAR-15 with me. I might still be in jail. In remembering this incident, the prayer of the great Army Lieutenant General Hal Moore in "We Were Soldiers Once and Young" comes to mind: "Oh, yes, and one more thing, dear Lord, about our enemies, ignore their heathen prayers and help us to blow those little bastards straight to Hell. Amen."

16

MOVIES AND MOVIE STARS

I am friends with many actors, and consider many others casual acquaintances. I am not a big-name movie star, but I'm often mistaken for one. People stop me on the street and in restaurants to ask if I am a star and I say, "Well, I have been fortunate enough to have been cast in about 25 films, many of them big-name, but I am just a big guy with a little part," which usually gets a laugh.

"You should be in movies," Oliver Stone remarked upon meeting me for the first time in 1985. He cast me in the first "Wall Street," trying, without success, to "loosen" me up in my acting scenes and finally giving up. "Chuck," he impatiently explained, "you are too damn stiff. However you are the perfect anthropomorphic prop." I accepted that. I guess one could say I had the look but not the talent. I never had a great desire to be a movie star anyway, but it would have been fun and I would, undoubtedly, have a ton more money.

I appeared in both "Wall Street" movies, "Nixon," "Fast Food and Fast Women," "Basquiat," and "Boomerang." Tom Cruise might still be in his wheelchair in "Born On The Fourth of July" if I, as a Secret Service agent, hadn't picked him up. I have been a limo driver, bodyguard, Frenchman, and Captain Gentile in "Night Falls On Manhattan." I have been directed by some of the better-known directors in the business: Oliver Stone, Sidney Lumet, the Hudlin Brothers and Julian Schnabel, also an excellent painter. I have a huge Schnabel, simply and aptly titled "C," that he gave me for my 50th birthday. Norman Mailer tried to get a big part for me in the movie titled, "Tough Guys Don't Dance," based on his novel, but the lead actor, Ryan O'Neal, was having no part of me, and a friend of his was cast instead. That was okay because the movie wasn't a real success, even with O'Neal's talent and notoriety.

Oliver Stone is a long-time friend. Maybe I should say "was" because he threw Paige and me out of his LA home. One night I got upset when one of Oliver's friends made a pass at Paige in front of me. That was a very bad thing to do. He should not have pushed my buttons, especially when I had had too much to drink. I grabbed the man and pushed him to the floor and threatened to hit him with a beer bottle, and yelled, "I am going to kill you!" Oliver knew I was not fuckin' around, remembering his own Vietnam days. The next morning at breakfast, Oliver's wife said, "You are going to have to leave. Oliver thinks you're crazy." Oliver was right. Paige and I spent the rest of our LA trip at the Beverly Hills Hotel.

One movie star friend's wife, who we mistakenly thought had retired for the night, also threw me out when she caught her husband and me playing Russian Roulette. A scene fit for a horror movie ensued and I do not blame her. It is a dangerous game and we might have killed each other although I doubt if the gun was even loaded. I won't mention names.

I traveled all over Europe with Oliver. We were in Paris in November 1989 when the buzz was going around about the potential fall of the Berlin Wall. We decided to fly over to Berlin to see what was happening and to check out the nightlife. We expected some real excitement, but the nightclub scene was boring, lifeless, dull and pedestrian. We did not stay there too long. Oliver remarked, "guess we have been in Los Angeles and New York too long."

We hit the bars again right after the Wall's demise, figuring the Germans would be going haywire by now, but that was not the case at all. Seems we were more excited than most of the people in the clubs. There was a quiet acknowledgment of the "Wall's" fall, an acceptance rooted in a "what do we do now?" kind of shock, I later thought. Now, they could travel from East to West Berlin and rejoin loved ones and their lives had just been changed, or perhaps reverted, and life would go on as if nothing had ever happened except the passage of time. There were quiet tears, but certainly not the unbridled jubilation we had expected. We both started home with pieces of the Wall, I with two pieces, but on the flight home a good-looking stewardess talked me out of the smaller piece. I do not know what Oliver did with his. I removed my piece from its place in my safe when I began writing this book. I wanted to look at it. I rolled it over in my hands, recalling its historical significance.

Michael Nouri, an accomplished musician, and I have spent time in Central Park sitting on the ground singing and playing our guitars for anyone who wants to listen. Admirers sit on the slopes nearby, listen for a little while, finally recognizing Nouri, and can not believe what they are seeing. But this is New York and anything that can happen, happens here, but doesn't necessarily stay here unlike Vegas. Occasionally, people drop money in our guitar cases. Once, I think we had $26, but we do not play for money. We do it because it is fun. Everything, every bit of it is, and has been, great fun. I value all my friendships that have endured over the years.

Taki Theodoracopulos, and I were guests of the "Oprah Show" many years ago when she did a segment called "Older Men Who Date Young Women." I know a lot about that subject. Taki loves to tell, and retell, the story of our flight to Chicago and our appearance there: "Chuck is walking up and down the aisle of the plane, blazer thrown over his shoulder, silk handkerchief in his pocket, saying in a sing-song manner, 'I'm going to be on the Oprah show! I'm going on the Oprah show!' One young lady, who'd heard enough, looked up from her book, rolled her eyes at Chuck, and pointedly and loudly asked, 'Who cares?' That shut Chuck up for a little while.

"Seated on the stage with Oprah, she pasted on her rapt-attention, solicitous, and caring look. Chuck, who had a few drinks on the plane, was in his usual too-many-drinks overbearing self. A lady in the audience, who has been listening to all the bullshit for way too long, yells. 'I wouldn't want you taking my daughter out.' Chuck, being a quick rebounder in any situation, flashed a smile, and replied, 'Madam, I wouldn't want to take your daughter out.' The audience howled, but I recall that Oprah was not too happy. We were not invited back."

During the 80s and early 90s, I gained a reputation as a ladies' man and bon vivant. I appeared on many TV talk show: "Regis and Kathy Lee," "Geraldo Rivera" and "Current Affair," where the usual subjects were Vietnam and "man about town." I loved the notoriety and attention. It was heady stuff then. I spent a lot of time at "Elaine's" and met many friends I have kept throughout my life. At Elaine's, I had a lot of fun and where I could be myself for a while. Elaine Kaufman described me thus: "Chuck is a lot of fun and a playboy from the old school." I did my best to live up to my reputation.

17.

MOTORCYCLES AND THERAPY

I rode a motorcycle all over Germany, but sold it before I left the Army, and bought a Triumph Bonneville when 1 got home in 1969. I loved English bikes, but I finally settled on Harleys and rode the hell out of them. My favorite was a Super Glide Harley, a truly beautiful bike. I loved that cycle, protecting and guarding it like it was worth a million dollars. It was always waiting for me and it never let me down. I'd hit the starter button, peel out of the garage, and create a burst of air that sent flying any paper, cigarette butts, or dog poop lying on the sidewalk that Buddy Kahn said I could probably have sold. I was ready to raise some hell all over Manhattan. Stop me, you ingrates! Remember, this was 1969, I was just back home, but sometimes I was still in Vietnam. I did not appreciate being unappreciated by the populace for being a Vietnam veteran. It would take me a little while to assimilate.

I hit the bars the first part of most nights, picking up the best looking girls. Before my partying got totally out of control, the cream of the belle monde would, at any given time, be on the back of my bike both arms holding tight around my body. We sped up Park Avenue at about 80 miles an hour, usually well after midnight without helmets, our hair flying in the wind and our clothing plastered to our bodies. It was fun, dangerous, and sexy. Soon though, my reputation as a wild man, drinker and cocaine user, preceded me. No one would even think about getting on the Harley with me. The ladies still liked the image, though, and I still had no shortage of the most beautiful women in the city. I am not giving names.

Finally, it was just me and my bright red Harley, playing cat-and-mouse with the East side potholes, flashing by high-rise apartments, bars, the homeless, and rich couples or lovers, on their way home from late-night clubs and hook-ups. People who live in New York City are tough and blasé. It takes a lot to get their attention for more than a second or two, so I am sure no one was surprised at seeing a streak of red on its way uptown.

Now, I consider all this as my way of daring anyone to confront me. I was a Vietnam survivor and tired of being treated like an outcast because of it. I knew I was going to suffer for the rest of my life, from time to time, with flashbacks, and from real and imagined injuries and illness. I would be on my way to the emergency room of Lenox Hill Hospital in the middle of the night because my leg ached, my stomach hurt or I could not sleep. I would be in "can do" mode most of the time. I would not be able to convince myself I was okay, and that maybe I was just getting old.

Naturally, I did not see it that way at first. Then it was something else completely. Then it was my Vietnam therapy, freedom and power. I could be 20 again, not completely innocent, but with no knowledge of war except what I read in the newspapers or heard and saw on TV, which was not much. I could tell myself I had never been to Vietnam and that it was all a nightmare, but I could not convince myself. The pain was there to remind me lest I tried to forget.

On my cycle, I could fling my emotions out onto Park, Madison and Fifth Avenues and let them bounce off the traffic lights, concrete barriers, benches where people passed the time in the noon sun, and the pink and yellow tulip beds. Feelings or memories never make a dent. They are only individually felt, and I could rid myself of some of my darkest ones for a little while with no one the wiser. Those memories could land wherever they liked. I find it a little difficult to understand, but it is a good description. I consider all this my PTSD therapy. There would be years of more therapy to come.

I have been under the careful eye of a New York City psychiatrist since the late 70s. He says he is getting too old to hear all my crap, but I still go, pay $250 for my 50-minute hour, spill my guts, and he still listens. "That is what I'm here for," he says, nodding. He leans back, closes his eyes and listens, interposing quiet questions and comments. I am not sure if he is sleeping or listening, but he is not the patient, and as long as I keep talking, it is okay. I explain to him as best I can my feelings of insecurity, even though, intellectually, I know I am okay. We examine my fear of failure, of having not accomplished anything significant, not having the approval of my friends or their not acknowledging my achievements. I think sometimes they have not met me or known me as I really am. I am not sure I even know the real me. Deep down, I might, but it is difficult to be truly sure and even more difficult to find me. When my shrink asks, "Who do you think you really are?" in that usual psychiatrist way, quietly and probingly, he is asking me something I can't answer.

"I don't know," I reply. "I can transform into different personalities depending on the situation: man about town, rich man, know-it-all, brash and subdued, depressed, elated, sad to the point of tears without reason, and prone to speak without thinking. I love my wife and I tell her so often, but other times I am nasty and downright mean with my words. Who the hell is the real me? I realize most of my perceptions are not based in reality, but it is hard to conquer. The doctor listens. He does not counsel me with words I want to hear, but with words I need to hear. They remain with me for a while. Usually before our sessions end, he is leaning toward me and we engage in animated and sometimes heated conversation. Over the years, we have become a little more than doctor-patient. I know him, but he knows me better. If anyone is able to penetrate your inner core, they know you a whole lot better perhaps than you know yourself. That is my psychiatrist.

As for therapy, it is not always the psychiatrist who heals. There is someone to whom I owe a great deal: Ted Raymond, well-known North Shore Boston financier and Yale man. I met Ted many years ago and he recognized that indefinable look in my eyes, sadness, fury, helplessness, and devil-may-care attitude. Somewhere along the way, I had forgotten how to feel, how to release the softer side of myself, and how to relate to, or even how to trust, another person. Ted sensed, somehow saw, I had been through some kind of hell, and he seemed to understand. He invited me out to his farm for weekends and I would ride my Triumph bike out there, its engine whining and its tires thumping on the pavement. I loved the sounds. I convinced myself I could conquer the world, and yet I had just returned from a part of the world I could not conquer, and I was not yet able to reconcile that fact. Ted gave me a job. He put me to work on his farm in Ipswich, Massachusetts. I mucked stalls, hoed vegetables, rode horses and cut grass. Mundane and boring work, these chores allowed me to relax in the calm atmosphere. There, I began to purge my troubled self of disturbing pictures that sometimes popped into my mind unexpectedly. My thoughts, views and perceptions of life began to change. It was great therapy, and I am grateful to Ted for his insight into my psyche and his valuable and appreciated help and friendship. When I bought my first Harley, I made a gift of my Triumph Bonneville to Ted.

One of my friends sat me down one night: "Chuck," he began, "you have a swagger like no other. When that six foot three broad-shouldered frame moves, people stop and stare. You drape that couture blazer over your shoulders and, with that old-fashioned movie-star face, what else is a person to do? You are cocky, confident, rich and handsome. You have it all, and yet in the midst of all this, you seemingly want to destroy your life. You have sunk into a dark abyss of cocaine and alcohol that will eventually take you down. I've known you for a long time and I don't believe you want to live this way anymore. Nobody wants to return your phone calls or be around you because you have become obnoxious. Sooner or later, you're going to kill yourself or someone else. You've got to get into rehab and quick." I heard, but did not listen, and continued my lifestyle and my therapy, but deep down, I acknowledged the truth.

The 1980s were my years of wine and roses. I sank into depression, rose to elation, and spent a lot of time in between. I had discovered cocaine, that all-consuming, make-me-feel-invincible thing that kept me up most of the night and got me up in the mornings wanting more. I was functioning in the work place, although I cannot imagine how, but I became more successful than ever. I thought all my friends were wrong. I had found the magic potion. In reality, the magic potion had found me and was extremely reluctant to let me go. It took a while for me to let it go. Ultimately, I followed the advice of many friends and checked myself into rehab. Most of my caste wound up at Betty Ford or Hazelden clinics, but I sat out my self-imposed exile for four days in a Long Island drunk tank for Scots-Irish cops and criminals. I left with phone numbers of "buddies" and local AA and NA groups.

18.

NELL'S AND 1629

One evening, Norman, Oliver Stone, Willem Dafoe and I went to Nell's on 14th Street in Manhattan, New York's "hottest" hot spot, without a worry about getting past the Velvet Ropes. Michael Douglas may have been with us, but I am not sure. The place was packed as usual, but we knew we would get a booth. Cliff, the manager, zeroed in on us, trying to pull himself together at seeing two tough guys: an actor and a movie director. I suspect he was more impressed by Norman than by the rest of us. Calmly, and with the greatest aplomb, he approached a table where the singer/actress Annie Lennox, was seated. "I need to move you," he discreetly told her, in his best Jamaican accent, "I'll give you a good place a little farther back." Annie was furious and for a few minutes, the shit hit the fan. Other patrons were trying to get a look at what was happening. Finally, she shoved back her chair, tossed her head, got up and followed him to a new table, throwing a few more choice words at Cliff and a glare at us.

It was not this night at Nell's, but later on Halloween night, that I pulled a "Dead Bug." Suddenly, I was not at Nell's. I was in Saigon with my SOG buddies. After I dropped to the floor yelling "Dead Bug!" I was joined on the floor by another man, yelling "Dead Bug! Dead Bug!" I was wearing a round pumpkin costume and could not roll over enough to get up, so the two of us just lay there until someone lent us a hand. We caused quite a commotion and nearly got thrown out. To the vast number of wall-to-wall customers, this was a sight they had never witnessed. Two grown men, one a pumpkin, lying on their backs, waving their arms and legs in the air was astonishing and even entertaining. Later, the other man introduced himself to me. He had been in a different location in Vietnam, but he knew all about "Dead Bug." Since he was the last man down, he bought me two more rounds. We reminisced and promised to stay in touch.

Someone during the evening, one of our group said I should open a bar. "That way," he said, "You can save a lot of money." I had actually been talking with a good fireman friend, Terry Quinn, about that idea for a while.

Terry and I opened 1629 at the corner of 84th and Second Avenue in Manhattan. We opened in the early 90s, without a clue about the liquor business, nor the long hours and sweat we would need to expend in making it successful. Up until then, all I knew about how to run a bar was to sit in one and order Jack Daniels brought to my table. Ostensibly, we modeled 1629 after Elaine's, where customers had their own tables. Retrospectively, I do not know what overtook me and convinced me to open a bar, but I image it was because I was an alcoholic. What could get better than that? However, it was a place where I met a lot of friends and learned a lot about myself.

Terry and I lasted about a year and a half until we could not take it any more. I recalled Taki's warning when I told him I was buying a bar. He just had to remind me that we were getting too old to stay out too late at my, or anyone else's, bar.

One night Taki, and our great friend, Billy David, an advertising man and war hero, were at their table, and a couple of guys pointed toward them laughing. Billy David, being a little over the limit, walked over. "What's so funny, tough guys?" he demanded. "What is so damn funny? Maybe you would like to tell me. Right here. Right now." The situation quickly escalated, and the whole place erupted in a fist-throwing, chair-breaking, all-out brawl. Taki, not to be left out of anything as exciting as a brawl, and also with a bit too much liquor, stood up, grabbed a customer by the collar, and yelled at the top his voluminous voice, "Run! Run for your lives!" I could always count on those two to get something going. No one was seriously hurt and the police did not arrive. They were already there, out of uniform in the middle of the brawl, and enjoying it as much as everybody else. By night's end, everyone had settled down and wound up buying drinks for each other.

The bar ran the gambit of customers on any given night: Vietnam veterans, FBI agents, cops, Mafia wise guys, actors, models, football players, firemen, Hells Angels and the Irish Mafia, the "Westies," headed up by Jimmy Coonan and Mickey Featherstone, one of whom later went to jail and the other went into the witness protection program. Sometimes, early in the evening, some of Gotti's people showed up, as well as the New York City Mayor. Each group sat at its own table, each buying the other tables Jack Daniels, beer, or whatever their favorite drink was, each talking, laughing and having a hell of a time, while trying to be heard over the blues and the country and western music.

1629 had a reputation as a tough-guy place, but we rarely, if ever, had any serious problems because our guests knew they could not "fuck around" there. That is unless Taki and Billy David happened to be there. Women did not frequent 1629 much, except as invited. The Hells Angels usually showed up after midnight, their shiny top-of-the-line cycles of all colors, lined up around the block, guarded by a couple of the younger members. The HA conducted themselves better than anyone, and they held their annual New York get-together at 1629, to which they brought their ladies, and Wilt Chamberlain. If you never saw Wilt Chamberlain walking through a door, towering above everyone, you missed something.

Chuck Zito, (former New York President of Hells Angels and cast member of the movie "Sons of Anarchy") frequented 1629, and was introduced to me by a friend, Mickey Rourke. A framed 4'x6' poster of Chuck hangs in my entryway. The poster does not mean a lot, since they can be bought online at a reasonable price. What makes my poster special is the writing in the upper left corner: "To Chuck. Good luck and best wishes. Love and respect. Chuck Zito Hells Angels

World."

Once leaving 1629 in the early morning hours, a homeless, rumple-clothed, man was begging on a nearby step. He saw my military field jacket and my Army boots, which at that time I always wore. The man stumbled to his feet and fixed his bleary eyes on me, and rubbed them as if not believing what he saw. "Daiwi, Daiwi," he said almost reverently. He looked me straight in the eyes and raised his hand in a soldier's salute. I was taken aback for a minute, but raised my hand in a return salute. His pain and despair were palpable. I felt it almost as mine. I reached into my pocket and placed a wad of money into his hand. I do not know how much it was, but I did not need it. I suddenly knew, though, what I did need. I recognized what I had to do to get back on my feet. It had been much too long. The next morning, I arose earlier than usual and rode my Harley down to Washington to visit The Vietnam Veterans Memorial, or "The Wall." As I rolled along, I wondered if I might be able to release some of my grief and anxiety.

Apprehension hit me as I approached The Wall. My fingers finally found and traced the names of *Rolf E Rickman, Paul D Potter, Donald W Welch, Charles Norris, Richard E Pegram, Jr., Tadeusz M Kepczyk, Donald R Kerns, Gilbert A Secor, Harold R Voorheis, Talmadge H Alpine, Jr., James T Kickliter, Robert J Uyesaka, Howard S Varni and William H Bric III,* most of my fellow Green Berets who died on August 23, 1968. There were three more fellow Green Berets, whose names I did not find, but they were not forgotten. Thousands of names of friends, husbands, brothers, fathers, and lovers were etched into that wall, and it suddenly became all too real. My name could very well have been there too and someone might have been searching for it. I was there though, alive and able to grieve. My pain was raw, real and angry. I was not weeping for myself, but for them. Salty tears trickled down my face and I broke down and wept openly and unashamed. I was not alone.

Reluctant to leave, I stopped for a few minutes at the site of "The Three Soldiers" statue as a tribute to those dead and those still alive who had served in that seemingly never-ending war. I bowed my head in sorrow and honor. When I finally left the Wall, I left no note, poem or photo as many others did. My fallen comrades did not need them and I knew I would not either. I would always be able to close my eyes and see them, young, eager and laughing as if their lives would never end.

I spent many evenings thereafter putting together the remnants of my life as a Vietnam soldier. I realized that the best and brightest part of me was and always would be a soldier. I was a man bound by a code of behavior so instilled in my core I could never betray it.

19.

TRAVEL THROUGH OLD HAUNTS

From 1969 to 1993, twenty-five years post Vietnam, my friends and I were in frequent discussions about the war and the MIAs. Our questions went unresolved. At first, the idea was fleeting: Maybe I should revisit and document Vietnam, and particularly Hanoi. In 1993, my idea became a reality.

I traveled back to Hanoi, along with my girlfriend, Paige Hall, working under the auspices of Esquire Magazine" and "Current Affair." I intended to get an interview with General Vo Nguyen Giap, the renowned North Vietnamese General. General Giap began his military and political career in 1940 and came into prominence during World War II. He was Commander-In-Chief of the Vietminh, a Communist-dominated nationalist movement formed in 1941. This movement fought for independence from French rule and later most of its members joined the Viet Cong. During his career, he was responsible for defeating the French and Chinese armies. There was still a question whether he had defeated the United States, as well. That depended upon whose point of view one believed. General Tom Needham of the POW and MIA recovery effort was also on my interview list, but did not happen. I was there, too, perhaps out of curiosity as to why I may have more in common with the Vietnamese than my own former officers. I did have inklings, though. I was looking for a counterpart, someone from the other side to help me understand who, what, or even why, I was fighting there in 1968. It now seemed so obscure and unanswerable.

PTSD does not disappear. It lies dormant, but ready to surface at any time. During my trip, my sleep was often disturbed by images of bullet-riddled bodies in tortured positions, eyes wide open, watching and haunting me. I saw their mangled and dismembered limbs hanging like raw meat in a freezer. NVA commandos holding ready-to-fire explosives chased me. I felt the blood spurt on my face and body as I shot them, seemingly moving in slow motion. I awoke bathed in sweat, reached for a drink and the memories were temporarily assuaged. I knew they would not be gone for long.

On our fifth day in Hanoi, we had Nguyen, a Communist liaison, called a minder, from the National Press Office, who ensured I heard nothing but the Communist Party line. *You lost a war, we won freedom. You lost 60,000 soldiers, we lost two million people. You fought for politics, we fought for our culture. You have many books and movies about the war, but all hide why you lost.* Nguyen, an inscrutable woman, seemed impervious to my impatience, born out of my disdain for the painful memories Hanoi evoked.

It was all Ivy League men and West Pointers then at the three-star Pullman Hotel in Hanoi's Old Quarter. I saw them morning 'til night, trading pedigrees and business cards against the backdrops of string quartets at breakfast tea in the lobby. Filipino chanteuses warbled "I'm Your Venus" over beady-eyed cognac drinkers, bankers, corporate liaison officers, higher-ups from the MIA team, and Lever Brothers marketers in the evenings. Most were there on convention and dressed for Pebble Beach. Even the journalists were Ivy League, not the hellfire dropouts with Nikons who walked point next to me in '68.

In a few hours, I would roll out of bed and visit the breakfast shops on Le Van Hu Street, where I downed bowls of hyper-spicy soup to clear my head. Sometimes it helped, and sometimes not. I usually had no clue what my day would bring. I rifled my briefcase several times a day looking for the assignment letters from "Esquire" and "Current Affair," always halfway convinced they might not be there. I was introduced as an American journalist/former soldier, probably the first to come back to Vietnam to report the country's changes since the Vietnam War. Paige carried the video equipment "Current Affair" gave us, so we at least looked like media.

Except for the nightly four-hour binge, I could not hide the fact that, this time around, I had brought nothing to this country except a midlife crisis that was fast approaching a possible breakdown. I realized I had become not a commanding officer, but that I had become "second in charge" to my desire to succeed and overcome my memories of combat. If I had dug deep enough into my soul, I could find excuses for that, although none of them would hardly make sense. Why and how, I wondered, did that turncoat Marine, whom I was meant to find and kill in one of my first Vietnam missions, know my name but I did not know his. How was that possible? Were we not the ones who always had the answers?

I cried one morning, my first tears in a long time, at a communal breakfast with some Australian press guys at the hotel. Actually, I broke down: 15 minutes of uncontrollable sobs. I could not say for sure what caused the breakdown, except to say it was a combination of factors. Maybe it was the hotel, the incessant chatter or stupid questions, at least to me, from the press guys, or my increasing inability to deal with people. *What the hell are they all going on about? Do they not realize I was there in 1968, fighting for freedoms most of them may never even thought about or simply taken for granted? Do they not know there were times I questioned my own government and sometimes even myself? Can they not see my invisible scars?*

I had been in a state of panic since I saw Hanoi rising up out the window of the Cathay-Pacific 90-seater from Hong Kong. It was an overwhelming panic, not the adrenaline kind I had spent a decade learning to harness. I felt this one deep inside, like an invading cancer, born of guilt, terror and rage, and I could not distinguish one feeling from the other. They were just one big hurt rolled into one.

The sight of old bomb craters below started me off. They made the landscape look like some urban golf course, though with sand and water in places they had no topographical reason for being. My West Point classmate, Bobby Jones, was shot down by a MIG-17, creating some of that lunar real estate. Bobby told me the pilot had circled and dipped as if to say *Got you.* Bobby was captured and spent nearly seven years in the Hanoi Hilton.

My panic got worse as the 90-seater's door opened, and I felt that 25-year old heat and fear. I was wiping mist off my sunglasses when Paige nudged my arm. Four men were doing the flat-footed jungle run across the tarmac toward us, the only non-Asians off the plane. They were just customs guys, but Christ, I was brought back: the mustard-brown uniforms, the red stars on their lapels, the cheap, sturdy work boots, and the four-to-one ratio. And that look: the single-digit body fat, that blind but intelligent obeisance, those 40-years-old faces that did not look a day over 15.

I always had a game-face for these people and I wondered why I did not anymore. For the first time, I questioned why I ever had it. My credentials were always so unimpeachable: socially, from birth, as a soldier, from WP on, and as an American, from an assurance of victory. When I was medevaced out to Japan at Christmastime '68, with wounds, but mostly with malaria, there was no doubt the war was winnable, and soon.

Every shop I passed seemed to nullify me. I was nothing, invisible, passe and worthless. Every drop of their lousy soup seemed to challenge my essence. Why could I not accept that this City, this Hanoi, was and always would be, a component of that destiny sealed so long ago? Was this what I had unknowingly signed on for so many years before? Every man, woman and child looked at me like they owned me. In my heart, I agreed with them. They did own me, and I had to find a way to negate that. Nothing in '68 was this personal, this warlike, this defeating, and this scary. I could no longer paint the town of Hanoi red. That time was long past.

Two days out of Hanoi, as we crossed the Hein Luong Bridge, Nguyen leaned into the back of the rented 10-year-old Toyota and gave me one of her now familiar, slight smiles. "We just crossed into the former Demilitarized Zone," she said, her eyebrows rising just a little, as if to signify ominousness, or perhaps blame. The problem was, I knew the look - the look of blame that I had not been able to release or forget. I reminded myself I had no blame. My government sent me to do a job and I performed all my duties to the best of my ability, even though I often used some of those elite abilities for things, looking back, that maybe I should not have. But what was I supposed to do 25 years later? Was I expected to apologize to every person in the damned country? I doubted Paige, who sat beside me in the sweltering heat, had ever heard of the DMZ. Why would she? She had never been in Vietnam and she sure as hell had never been to war.

We smiled at Nguyen like tourists who have just been told the Grand Canyon is out the left-hand window. I was sure Nguyen noticed our smile and interpreted it as attempting to divert her guilt-inducing attitude. She was a very smart Communist, and I was keenly aware she knew exactly what her attitude projected.

I had been dry for the past two days and I asked Paige to light a cigarette for me. I needed something in my hand, or anything that would give me assurance I had done the right thing.

Nguyen had not stopped. "Here in Quang Tri Province" she said, "they lose a man every day to unexploded ordnance and buried mines. One day, one farmer," she continued, rolling her eyes. Mostly Viet Cong weapons, I thought: *two-charge Bouncing Betties set to explode at waist level, sending shrapnel in every direction, and booby-trapped V40 Mini-Fragmentation Grenades called Mini-frags, their pins partially pulled 25 years ago. How could I forget Toe Poppers, those 3.5 ounce, drab olive-colored Anti-Personnel mines?* Lacking conventional weapons, the NVA ingeniously used these weapons designed for maiming and killing. I can only imagine the number of maimed soldiers who returned home after coming into contact with them. I see the injured in my eyes-wide-open sleep. I certainly did not need a Communist to remind me.

Just before dusk, we stopped at a beach town so Paige and Nguyen could swim. The beautiful evening calmed me as I sat in the sand with Tran, our driver, trading his fractured English with my Vietnamese. Paige is six-feet tall and a former New York City ballet dancer. Out of the water, she put on a white linen dress and danced en pointe in the setting sun, and soon the town came out to watch. She was beautiful and tan, and the wind slightly lifted her hair as she danced. The sand shifted beneath her agile feet. I, who had seen her in just about every mode, was in awe of her beauty and grace.

We may have been the only whites the Vietnamese had ever seen. One chain-smoking man in his 50s, whom I pegged as a former NVA, sat cross-legged and began talking to me, less freely, it seemed, after Nguyen joined us to translate.

"You Special Forces?" he finally asked. "Green Beret?"

I nodded, glancing down at my Banana Republic journalist-wear, and suddenly felt ridiculous in it. It was cocktail hour and I was jonesing. I took the last pull on the cigarette and flipped it off into the sand.

"I fight here," the man said, pointing north up the beach to seaside cliffs. "Inside was a huge bunker complex in which NVA troops moving south were organized. How long was your tour?"

"Nine months." I replied, pausing a moment. "I would like to visit that complex some time," I said a little off-hand, trying to pretend it did not matter. Nguyen seemed to sneer as she looked at the man. "Nine months," she needlessly translated, "and he wants to see the bunker complex." I had her figured for a misandrist, but thought maybe not. She seemed to like the man, who I thought might be her father. I later learned he was.

He nodded, calculating, and pointed to parts of his

body. "You wounded bad, yes?"

"Yep."

"Still bad?"

I nodded pointing to my head. Self-consciousness stole over me halfway through the gesture, meant to signify the delirium of falciparum malaria, the wound that eventually demobilized me. He did not understand that I had tried to convey I had malaria, and he looked at me quizzingly. Nguyen translated again, "He said he had a head injury." She tapped the side of her temple with her delicate fingers.

"Malaria," I said, and she told the man. He nodded, now understanding, and I sat back on my hands and squared my shoulders to the ocean like a New Ager greeting the sunset. Too bad we were facing east.

"You kill us?" he asked.

"Sure," I said. "Sure I did."

I turned away from his eyes, now recalling mines, and my inner fears I had not shook of being wounded, paralyzed or disfigured, prospects much more random and open-ended than death, and maybe a lot more scary.

The man shook cigarettes to the top of his pack and leaned past our driver, Tran, motioning for me to take one. "You fight nine months," he said, as he leaned to light me up with an old, well-maintained Zippo, probably worth a couple hundred dollars to a collector. He smiled and tiny lines crinkled around his eyes like calfskin. "I fight ten years."

"My father fought ten years," Nguyen repeated, as

154

if I had bad hearing. The guilt I had been trying to still temporarily returned. I was sure Nguyen, in her adept way of instilling guilt, picked it up. I smiled at her, but I did not fool her. She knew and was pleased. I was not.

We were out of Hanoi on Highway One, a glorified name for a two-lane blacktop that led to unimproved country road for long stretches, up narrow switchback roads through green conical hills, skidding through potholes as we hugged the shoreline of the China Sea. In between, we drove through indistinguishable tiny towns between Quang Tri and Hue, Than Nhu, Hai Lang, Hianh Fan. Each had a government building, usually some Soviet Modern two-story affair in orange stucco, and a couple of shops: the "lom-lop" for tire repair, each seemingly the same, and a shanty cafe with no refrigeration, and a heady smell of vinegar, far more unpleasant than the heavy grease of American joints. Every building we passed had the smell of poverty and every third cafe had a dog tethered outside, barking and straining at its leash. It took a while, but I finally understood these were not pets, but the night's menu.

Scarecrows of old women in threadbare black dresses flagged us from cafe doors to entice us to stop in for a bowl of rice and nouc mam, a briny sauce made from rotted fish. Flesh hung off their bones. Prolonged chewing of areca nuts, commonly referred to as betel nuts, had blackened their teeth even the gold ones. They looked variously like the Oakland Raiders logo or the awful death's-head jewelry my Nungs used to wear on

155

gold chains. The beads they wore were carved of smooth ivory, like the skin on these women's faces, with inlaid eyes of cheap, low-karat gold that would turn black in the thick of the jungle heat.

When we stepped out to sightsee at the summit of Hai Van Pass, the border between Hue and Da Nang, I was struck by the beauty of the country. At 500 meters, the watery heat did not wash everything out at sea level, and the colors were spectacular, soft and saturated at the same time. The red-tile roofs of a half-dozen tiny villages folded into the emerald foliage below. The pastel collage of the China Sea became visible when the white-green ocean clouds rolled away. It was one of those epiphanies, like going through Provence the first time and realizing all those famous burnt-sienna, cubist hills of a Cezanne canvas are actually there. Even the haze was lime-green, like a replica of the watercolor landscapes on Chinese menus. It made the tiny black lines and white exhaust plumes of the planes flying out of an airport 25 kilometers ahead look truly intrusive, like western pencil smudges and erasures of the artist. This was particularly so for the planes flying west into a vast green valley. It might have been just cognitive dissonance. I never hit the Hai Van Pass in '68. Then it was Apache territory, somewhat like the long-forgotten U.S. badlands, but I was wondering how I could have missed this beauty so entirely. It was not just the altitude, because I had spent countless hours looking at the Hai Van over a Huey's skid as I flew up to Phu Bai or Khe Sanh. It was that then my mind was not on the beauty of the country, but rather, on trying to survive. I got so lost in my aesthetic/ecological reverie that it registered only slowly: *the international airport down there is, was, the old airstrip. And that is actually a series of valleys yawning to the west: Happy Valley, the A Shau, just visible past one of the mountain ridges. Beyond that must be Laos, maybe also visible on a perfect day, and that is Da Nang below.* I grew quiet, thinking of the past, and as we arrived at the People's Committee of Da Nang City, a three-story limestone structure with a mansard roof, Paige remarked, "I thought you were asleep, but I should have known." She said it with an understanding that I had not realized she possessed.

We were finally about to be free of Nguyen. No one bothered to explain that she was only chaperoning us to Da Nang. I was glad to be rid of her quasi-historical quips. Her portents had begun to chafe like sandpaper. The Russian Federation's Consulate General was down the block, a reminder of why we had been there in the first place: to fight the spread of Communism. "Without the war," I said to Nguyen, getting a tad portentous myself as we drove past, "I believe that would still be the USSR Consulate General." Suddenly, her English was insufficient to follow me. She left us with a quick half-smile and a nod.

I detect right away that there will be no "Nguyen" ballyhoo with our new minder, Luc, who I guessed was in his mid-40s. He had been a scout on the Ho Chi

Minh Trail, shuttling intelligence between Laos, NVA camps and Da Nang during the war. I wondered if he could be the counterpart I had been seeking. In '68, he could not have been more than 13 when he started scouting, and he had that look, that unmistakable flinty character forged by years of permanent struggle. I felt I was picking up the spore of '68. Luc's communication skills were as theatrical as Nguyen's without the programmed remonstrance and rectitude that she couldn't seem to go without. His ponderous silences and expressions masked emotions: apprehension, melancholy, sadness, mystery, power, and a not so well-hidden curiosity about Paige and me.

Nguyen had no idea what SOG meant, but Luc did. He knew all about us. He spent his youth watching our teams drop into the jungle. He knew of FOB-4, remembers when it was overrun, my final battle there, and thinks he may have driven past in '67. He knew the city very well then, the western part, not east across the bridge, which was ours, though he was a little hazy on the chain of command. He actually believed that General Lam, the ARVN commander, was my senior officer, and that I was of the opinion that the South Vietnamese were my allies, not to mention comrades.

General Lam, a senior military officer in the Army of the Republic of Vietnam, held several military positions, including Commander of the RVNAF Artillery Training Center and Commander of Artillery in I Corps. His last position was Commander-in-Chief of Army Corp 1 Forward Command. South Vietnam fell to the North Vietnamese (the fall of Saigon) on April 30, 1975. That day, according to his son, General Andrew Lam, was the last day his father wore his military uniform. He commanded a Navy ship full of Army officers to the Philippines. Near shore, he changed into a pair of jeans and a T-shirt. He then threw his gun into the Pacific Ocean and asked for asylum in the United States. He continued his education at Golden Gate University in San Francisco. He earned an MBA and became a bank executive. Lam is his family name. By Vietnamese custom, he should properly be called Quang Thi. I can only assume Lam was as eager as I to get away from the horrors of war.

As Luc drove across the Song Hai Bridge, I told him of an outdoor sport some Special Forces guys - not me - favored in 1968: edging ARVN soldiers and their bicycles, accidentally-on-purpose, off the side of the bridge. When I first got there, I was told the bridge was a "target-rich-environment," though the ARVN got the message and scurried off whenever Special Forces jeeps crossed. Those clean ARVN uniforms, unused weapons, and well-oiled bikes did tend to make me pretty furious, particularly if I had just come out of the jungle. And the very mention of General Lam's name took me right back to those still-vivid 1968 memories of how angry I had been almost all the time.

In Kham Duc, a dirt-poor Montagnard village, I, along with Luc, my party minder, and Paige, were accused of being spies and were arrested and tossed into jail by local Party officials. I had been without liquor for the better part of the day and I was definitely not happy. I began to shake, and I delivered a few choice words to the Party officials. And, as I have stated before, when I drink, I get mean, and when I need a drink and cannot get it, I get even meaner. They were not about to listen to any tough talk or abide any drunken rages from a previous invader. We were told that Kham Duc was a "highly sensitive area." I highly suspected that was false. I figured it gave the "tribunal" of six Party types the opportunity to wear their mustard-browns with red stars, deliberate our fate, and feel important for a few minutes. Luc said not to worry because he would have us out of jail by the end of the day and he did. We were released without further incident or charges, thanks to Luc's knowledge of the system, and more than likely, a bribe of some kind, that I did not want to know about. Before our release, I curled up on the dingy bed springs and, through a dark haze, thought about a load of things, including being in a locker room of the Meadow Club of Southampton with a good friend, Billy David, magazine publisher and former Marine Lieutenant, who had also served in Da Nang. He was telling me of the time a year earlier, when he was playing tennis at the Palm Beach Polo Club and missed his last ten backhands. Being a good tennis player, this was unusual. The entire far side of his left eye's field of vision was dark. A nearly forgotten 23-year old piece of shrapnel had begun to work its way out of his eye. Hearing this at the Meadow Club, I began to panic. I suddenly felt the exact same thing happening to me, not only emotionally, but also physically. I felt it real and painfully and began to hyperventilate and sweat. I covered my forehead and began to fall apart. I tried, without success, to assure myself there was nothing to worry about or to even diagnose, except PTSD.

"Get an ambulance," I yelled to the Club attendant. "I need an ambulance quick. I am dying." I spent the night in a Southampton, New York, hospital recovering from nothing except the boundlessness and constriction I felt in 1968, when I was not able to describe, confront, or even scratch, the surface of these direct-opposite feelings.

There in the Kham Duc jail, lying on the so-called bed, waiting for the promised release, I began to scratch the surface in total recall and I sweated it out. My "dying" in the Southampton Club was one of many such episodes. I may be riding along Park Avenue, alone or with friends, and I lose it. Something, maybe a backfire of a truck, the roar of a motorcycle engine or just summer heat, triggers an ingrained response. I duck and drop to the floor of a cab or car and cover my head, and begin to sweat. If I am walking, I dive into the nearest hiding place, while listening to the drone of helicopters, the unmistakable sound of F-4s, and feel the heat of Napalm. I see the rows of caskets in Da Nang and go over the names of the dead. The episodes usually do not last long. Anxiety and fear well up like a fountain of pain. I know this sounds unreasonable and hard to understand by anyone but me and thousands of other veterans.

Looking for something to remind me I had ever been back to Vietnam proved fruitless. Not one shred of our military presence was left east of the bridges. They were mostly for Australian and East German tourists, who crossed to get down to the old Marine R & R spot, China Beach. Busloads go over on the hour to sightsee at the city's main attraction, Marble Mountain, used to be Apache country to the south, right outside my FOB-4 back door.

Luc did not live downtown where we spent some time, but he knew what all the changes in the past 25 had wrought, and that was fortunate. I did not recognize anything. Minus the bright lights of a multi-billion-dollar war effort, the old city seemed provincial. Most street names had changed, and almost all traces of the war's great machinery had vanished from west of the river as well, particularly down by the magnificent deep-water harbor we widened, pontooned, and in which we had killed miners and sappers. It was now factories and new bridges. Only a few of the great colonial houses remained. The fishing weirs down along the cove to the south had vanished, removing much of the Eurasian patina that marked Indochina so indelibly for me. Freakishly enough, what was left looked like small-town America, though with little charm. I remembered a place that bled history. "Where are the great houses," I asked.

"Gone. No great houses left," he said, "but we rebuild. All modern now," he sighed, with a hint of sadness and pride.

"And what about all the fishing weirs? Do they not need to obstruct the tidal water anymore to catch more fish?"

"No," he said. "Not really."

I looked for the floating houses that had been supported by metal drums. People living in the houses made their living in the fish business, and raised fish in metal nets beneath their floating dwellings.

"All those floating houses?"

"Not so much now," he says, pointing to a number of Japanese tankers anchored in the harbor, probably the world's most environmentally-destructive sailors. "Big boats. Oil. Pollution." He shrugged, his sorrow mask back on and more visible now. Even though he was proud, I believe he was also grieving for what his country had lost.

On the way back, I realized I had avoided the east side of the river and I asked Luc to drive across the bridge. We passed China Beach, where an international surfing competition was underway, and we made it down to FOB-4, where I had spent so many miserable days and nights. It was a place where battles were fought, and a place that returned me to the bone-chilling effects of malaria, death, the sound of mortar fire, and gut-wrenching fear. It seemed a strange land, a place I had never seen or even ever been, yet one so familiar that I knew every inch of it. I looked around for something I remembered and there was nothing, except Marble Mountain. It hadn't evaporated and disappeared like everything else, and even if it had, I would always be able to see it in my mind's eye. I would always see a Vietnamese Army Camp, full of barefoot soldiers, with nothing but a poor stretch of beachfront across the road, rice and nouc mam shanties. Now the ground had been broken for a big hotel that would be up by 1995.

The old city was booming, to be sure, to the point of traffic jams, but only because of a new five-mile "City" across the Song Hai Bridge: the world's largest Command and Control Center, the war's second biggest airport, U.S. military support buildings, hospitals, ordnance houses, etc., that lined the China Sea highway, from Monkey Mountain up north to Marble Mountain, which was technically ours, but belonged to Charlie. Each week, we sent a team up the centuries-old steps hewn into the side of Marble Mountain, but we could never navigate or destroy it quick enough.

For some reason, still unknown to me except curiosity, I could not forget Marble Mountain, and I asked to sightsee inside this foreboding mountain where my enemies took refuge and used as a place to fire upon us. Why, I asked myself, do I want to dredge up memories of taking massive attacks from there? I had never been inside Marble Mountain, but was still curious about it. What we did not know in 1968 was the vast extent of the enemy's network of multiple caves and trails within the Mountain. We learned later they stored implements of war there. The Marines, who carried 106m recoilless rifles while stationed on the Mountain's ledges, were always in more danger than we knew.

As I stood at the site of former FOB-4, I nearly lost my composure. I could hardly speak. Words escaped me, for what I remembered was beyond words. Tears stung my eyes. I had not expected, nor was I prepared, to respond with such deep emotion. Recently, I watched the video Paige and I took on the 1993 trip and was reminded anew of that experience.

Five craggy mountain peaks comprise Marble Mountain. Each is named for its mineral compound, and has a temple or sacred building, a pagoda, perched on top. I learned the history of the marble and limestone "Marble Mountain" from a guide we hired halfway up the same steps to which I used to dispatch platoons on nightly missions. They carry Vietnamese folklore names: Kim (metal), Thuy (water), Mock (wood), Hoa (fire), and Tho (earth). The guide took us into the largest grotto, the Thuy, a massive cave where Buddhas stared at me and followed my every step. Stalactites of calcium carbonate reached down to touch me with their long bony fingers.

The echoes inside the caves and trails were deafening, and assaulted my core and my psyche in ways that I could not explain or even understand. "They are the voices of the dead," our guide told us. I nearly choked. The air was stifling and I had to get out.

20.

WOMEN IN MY LIFE

I never suffered from a lack of female companionship. Beautiful women - actresses, models, businesswomen - have always been numerous in New York City. I have been associated with quite a few. However, I never reached a point of being ready for a long-term relationship until I met someone I thought might be a possibility.

In the early 70s, when I had not been out of combat very long, I was, as usual, spending time at New York's nightclubs. I do not remember the name of the one where I met Jennifer O'Neill. I hit the "hot" ones and there were many. An acting buddy introduced me to Jennifer and I was smitten with her beauty. An instant spark was readily ignited and we spent the rest of the evening together. Upon leaving, I touched her shoulder and said, "I'll call you." She had given me an open invitation with that lovely smile, and she handed me her number. She was my female equal in both society and wealth, and had become one of Hollywood's hottest actresses after starring in the movie "Summer of '42." I suppose we had it all.

New York is an "out-on-the town, going-to-dinner" city and Jennifer and I always attracted a crowd of oohing and aahing people asking for autographs, staring at us, and chasing us down streets to get a quick look. Jennifer did not like that one bit, but she did understand it went with the territory and was gracious about all the fuss. It did not bother me. I loved the attention and was always looking for more. The relationship progressed pretty fast and we became engaged. In the ensuing weeks, however, we began to see the other in a truer light. She became a real person instead of a beautiful movie star. I was still fighting a real and remembered war in the same high-profile, scorched-earth and cold-blooded existence as in 1968, virtually without awareness or choice on my part. I often retreated into a world no one else could ever understand or even be invited to enter.

Reality did not enhance a relationship that was probably doomed anyway. It is true, I guess, that a red-hot fire rapidly burns itself out, leaving only ashes, and that is part of what happened with Jennifer and me. Also, I have learned since then that it takes two "whole" people, or at least one well-adjusted person, to make a relationship work, and this one was questionable at best. We parted company still as friends, but we never kept in touch or saw each other again. I have always wished her well. It was great while it lasted.

Shelley Gile:

Shortly after my breakup with O'Neill and still in my short, post-grieving stage, I was having a shrimp cocktail and a beer with Wayne Lachman, a former advertising great, at P. J. Clarke's in New York's upper East Side.

"What's with your love life?" he asked. When are

you and Jennifer getting married?"

"Not going to be a wedding," I answered. "We broke up two weeks ago. Just did not work out, so I guess I am available again."

"Forget about Jennifer O'Neill," he said. "I'll introduce you to my sister-in-law, Shelley." After meeting Shelley, I forgot about O'Neill. Shelley was, it seemed, what I had always been looking for. She not only worked at "Vogue," she looked like one of their models. One evening upon arriving at P. J. Clarke's, the doorman said to Shelley, "Good evening, Miss O'Neill." Shelley was not at all pleased with that greeting, but handled it in her usual gracious manner, and we laughed afterwards.

The doorman later told me he could not keep up with my lady friends. "Neither could I," I said, laughing, "until I met Shelley." She and I began another one of those red-hot relationships, but this one did not burn out until a lot of learning and living had passed. We had a huge and beautiful wedding in 1971 at the Chatham home of her parents in Cape Cod, Massachusetts. Her father was Vice President of Morgan Guaranty. I liked her parents a lot.

"Women's Wear Daily" wrote a piece titled "The Quality People," in which we appeared. We took a lot of ribbing about this. Everywhere we went, friends called out, "Here come the QP."

Our marriage was a pretty good one, and we were happy and excited when Shelley became pregnant. We attended Lamaze classes and eagerly looked forward to becoming parents. Shelley had felt perfectly fine, and the pregnancy progressed normally, but something had gone wrong and remained undetected.

After delivery, the doctor came to speak with me. I knew there was a problem by his facial expression and demeanor. I did not expect, nor was I prepared, to hear his words, and they hit me like a bolt of lightning. "Your baby is very ill. I'm very sorry, but it isn't possible for him to live very long. His kidneys and lungs are underdeveloped and he cannot breathe properly. There is nothing we can do." He placed his hand on my shoulder in a show of compassion. I composed myself as best I could. "How long?" I asked.

"An hour or two, maybe. It is hard to know for sure."

"Can we see him?"

"Yes, of course," he answered, turning to leave. Then he turned back. "Do you want me to tell your wife?"

"No, I'll do it."

Telling Shelley about the baby was one of the most difficult things I ever had to do, outside of the war, but how does one equate that? I think she already suspected something was wrong, but I never knew for sure.

Christopher Charles Pfeifer died about three hours after birth. I held our beautiful baby in our arms and cried. I have never believed that a man should be considered weak if he cries. I think it may be just the opposite. Our joy had suddenly turned to absolute and profound sorrow. Shelley was totally devastated and inconsolable, as was I. Afterward, we grieved together and we grieved apart. Life had dealt us a hard blow and from frustration and extreme pain, I searched in vain for someone, or something, to blame, knowing there was nothing or no one I could blame. I railed against the injustice and internalized my pain. It took me a long time to recover from this loss.

For a time, Shelley and I seemed okay, even closer, but without us being aware, it became more and more difficult to live together. There was no defining moment. We simply drifted apart in the aftermath of the emotional devastation. I pulled away from Shelley, and she pulled away from me, and we subsequently divorced in 1981, which often happens I am told. There is a sort of indefinable bond that keeps us in touch every once in a while, although we moved on a long time ago. I think there may always be a bond between two people who have had a child together.

The loss of Christopher and our relationship and subsequent divorce are nothing more than memories now, except the pain returns sometimes. My greatest regret and sorrow lie not in all the wrong things I did. It is not even about my cocaine and alcohol dependency. My biggest regret lies in not becoming a father. The ultimate experience in my life would have been, without question, rearing Christopher. All my military training and my private life have shown and taught me that there is a gleaning process. There are no favorites or special circumstances. Rather, one's life seems to be more of chance or, as I usually say, destiny. I have learned that I am not now, nor will I ever be, impervious to human emotion. I have lived it in war and have now experienced in civilian life what might be the worst kind of emotional suffering. Pain, full-blown and real, may be alleviated for a short time, but nothing or no one, can eliminate it for a lifetime.

Shelley and I were astute at recognizing the value of real estate investments and we bought a house on Flying Point Road in the Hamptons, built a house on the bay in the Hamptons and bought an apartment on East 79th Street in Manhattan. After our divorce, I lived in one of the Hampton houses, rented the other, and subsequently sold them both and invested in the Montana and South Dakota ranches that I still own. Lisa and I now visit as often as we can.

Paige Hall:

Paige and I liked each other, but I was still fighting in Vietnam and certainly was not "husband" material. I could not see myself ever being married again and I had hardened my heart to that possibility, and I was drinking heavily. As I stated, when I drink, I get mean, and often times I was not even in the present. Paige witnessed a lot of this and tried to help to no avail. We fought and made up, fought and made up, which was okay for a little while, but not in the long run. After Paige and I arrived back in New York City in May 1993, we appeared on several talk shows about the trip. Our relationship continued for a short time thereafter. In the end, she wanted more from me than I was able to give. It wasn't about whether I cared enough. It was about my inability to live with myself, or anyone else, and conquer my PTSD. At that time, I am certain that had we married, it would have ended in divorce. We have remained good friends.

I had a few unimportant romances. They were fun, but not lasting. Everyone who knew me well was totally convinced I would never marry again, but they were wrong. I had told myself that dozens of times, but fate managed to seek out and sneak into that tiny crack in my somewhat hardened heart and my warped mind that remained open after I managed to get "clean." Getting clean wasn't the easiest thing I ever did, but I could no longer deny what I was feeling.

Lisa Crosby:

I met Lisa Crosby, Ford model, actress and photographer, at a book signing party in 2001, that neither of us had wanted to attend. I considered these parties a bore, but my publicist said I should go, as I was still involved in the "business." I would probably have backed out had I thought anyone that I really liked would be there. I was not seeking a serious relationship.

Lisa had come to the occasion with her good friends, movie director Fred Schepisi, and his wife, Mary. I had never met Lisa, but I knew about her. We were both under contract to Ford Models, and I remembered her "Old Spice" commercial that ran during a Super Bowl game. That was a big deal back then and still is. Lisa did "Chanel" and "Revlon" beauty campaigns in Paris, appeared in almost every magazine in the country and did numerous TV commercials and a few movie parts. I certainly did not think she would one day be my wife.

She is probably the first, and maybe only, passenger for which the Concorde waited on the tarmac in Paris on one of its first flights to New York City. She and another model friend, Shaun Casey, went duty-free shopping, forgot the time and nearly missed the flight.

I walked into the party looking around to see if I knew anyone and then if anyone looked interesting. There was. Lisa possessed, and still does, an aura of beauty and pleasantness. I made a beeline for her and that was it. Thinking back to that first encounter, I believe I saw in her face old memories, or sadness, only in a different place, time and kind. Maybe I recognized something that reminded me of myself. Recovering alcoholics and drug abusers sometimes leave indelible marks on those who love us. I later learned that her father was a life-long alcoholic. The next day after we met, I sent her a huge bouquet of red roses. We have been together ever since. Defying the belief of my friends, Lisa and I were married in February of 2012. Lisa is honest and true and I am confident within my heart that she loves me for who I am, not for what I have, ever had, or have ever been or done. We promised to "love, honor and cherish" each other in sickness and health and I do not intend to break that promise, just as I am confident she does not either. Even though I may not acknowledge it in word, I am fully cognizant that I, sometimes, maybe a lot of the time, am not an easy person with whom to live or even love. It is a lot easier to fall in love than to stay in love, but I am now smart enough to allow myself to be loved and to love.

Lisa left the modeling world and became an amazing photographer of people and animals, particularly horses. However, she just recently returned to modeling and is under contract to Iconic Focus Models of New York City. Lisa is a wonderful woman and wife. I am fortunate to have her. There is never a day that goes by that I don't say to her, "I love you." Did I mention she's a great cook?

She described me as someone who constantly cleans, in "The Wild Purple Heart of Chuck Pfeifer," an article written for the "Observer." That is not exactly true, but it's close. I like dinner dishes cleared right away and my bed made just right. I blame it on my military training. She also said I have a heart of gold. Sometimes, maybe. I have tried much harder in my later years to show the emotions I was not able to express in my early life, but it isn't always so easy. As the great Hal Moore wrote in "We Are Soldiers Still," a good wife is far more precious than jewels. The heart of her husband trusts in her and he will have no lack of gain. She brings him good and not harm, all the days of her life." I was privileged to call General Hal Moore friend. I read his book, "We Were Soldiers Once and Young," and wrote a note telling him how much I liked it. He responded. A month or two later, he and his wife visited me in New York and we managed to see each other as often as possible. It would be close to impossible to pay him the homage he deserves. He lived an exemplary personal and military life and received so many awards and accomplished so much, it would be space-prohibitive to list them. Revered by the troops he commanded, he knew from whence they had come. Smart and determined, he fulfilled his ambitions, all the while maintaining his personal integrity. I am sure I am not the only one he inspired along the way. I have always tried to apply one of his favorite quotes to my own life, "...there is always one more thing you can do to increase your odds of success."

21.

PEACE AND QUIET

Our ranches in Montana and South Dakota afford Lisa and me a respite form the New York City scene, and we try to go there for several months every year. Our Norwich Terrier, Mikey, always accompanies us, as does one of my guitars. Our house in Montana sits atop a little knoll overlooking mountains and meadows that are often grazed by all manner of wildlife. Once, a large black bear attempted to get into the hot tub on the back porch.

We fish the beautiful Madison River that flows below our Montana home and Hebgen Lake, a short drive away. Hebgen Lake is well-known in southwestern Montana, due to the August, 1959, Hebgen Lake earthquake, or Yellowstone earthquake, that killed 28 people. We hike the "Papoose" trail about every day, and frequent the Grizzly Restaurant, the town of Ennis, and occasionally drive into Bozeman. The nearby Blue Moon Café in Cameron is a favorite hang-out, where sometimes I sing and play my guitar after having dinner. People sit on the benches along the wall, drink a beer, and listen and dance to the music of a regular performer and anyone who might want to sing or play. I particularly like "Montana," a song I wrote some years ago.

Some of the best pheasant hunting and trout fishing in the country can be found at our South Dakota ranch. Every fall, I invite a number of buddies to join me there to hunt and fish, hang out, have a few beers and tell old jokes. We all laugh as though we have never heard them before.

For the last several years, I have hosted a group of friends for a trip up to West Point's homecoming game. Eight of us plan to attend the Duke-Army game on November 11, 2017. Breathing hard and chiding each other for being slow as we make the steep ascent to the stadium, we become young at heart again. When I hear the whirl of the helicopters, and see the paratroopers gliding to the middle of the field, an old familiar thrill arises in me, even with the passage of time, and I want to start all over. I would forego Vietnam the second time around, though. I search for old friends, find some, and we are truly glad to see each other again. All the while, I am sure each of us is remembering those no longer among us.

Last year, a cadet turned to one of my guests and asked if he could understand why the quarterback threw the last pass, which was intercepted.

"Don't know," my guest answered.

"You ever play?" the cadet asked.

"A little."

The cadet had been talking to John (Mose) Mosely, one of Notre Dame's greatest football players, who most definitely knew how to play.

Every year, I host a Christmas party for my close friends in New York. I have made it a tradition to sing Montana at the luncheon. As I lift my guitar from its case, Taki bangs his head against the wall in mock frustration. "Oh, no, not again," he groans. I start singing, and in the second verse, I'm joined by a chorus of voices heard five blocks up Park Avenue.

Montana
VERSE ONE

Montana is a lady,
Who's as pretty as her pines,
Montana is a lady,
Whose waters taste like wine,
Montana is my new love
Her green valleys I caress,
And her big sky holds her mountains,
Draped in lofty wilderness.

VERSE TWO

Montana loves her children,
That roam her free and wild,
The mule deer and the coyotes,
And all creatures meek and wild,
And the eagle flies above her,
And the big trout run her streams,
And the elk herds and the grizzlies
Play where man is never seen.

VERSE THREE

But changes are comin',
To the valleys fair and wide,
'Cause rich folks and their condos,
Force a need to subdivide,
But Montana is still a lady,
Who will not take the fall,
For the greed and love of money,
Will make her rise above it all.

CHORUS

And the rivers touch the mountains,
And the mountains touch the sky,
And the big sky bares the beauty,
Of the sweet by and by.

I wrote Paddy Brown in memory of Paddy, a fireman
friend killed on 9/11. I don't sing it often.

Paddy Brown

VERSE ONE

Paddy Brown was a man who knew no fear,
Just tall and proud in his bunker gear,
Whether in the Nam smokin' out VC,
Or charging up the stairs with Ladder 3.

VERSE TWO

Legends were told of Paddy and his men,
And all the boys that went back again,
They taunted death as they finally met,
America's heroes we will never forget.

VERSE THREE

At the WTC on that fateful day,
Paddy was there to show the way,
He took his boys to the 40th floor,
When everyone thought they could go no more.

CHORUS

Silver Star in the USMC,
Paddy was meant for history,
His heroism knew no boundary,
A legend to all in the NYFD.

When I heard the news on 9/11, I rushed to Ground Zero to help in any way possible. Right in front of my eyes, two people jumped and hit the ground. I watched in horror. I left and went to a triage center on Manhattan's West Side to help with injuries, but none came in. On that tragic day, it was outright death, and I'm still outraged.

I am quite certain if wars were actually fought by old men, there would be no wars, but they are not. Wars are fought by the young - mere boys and girls by an old man's standard, and what do they know? Do they know what it means to kill and possibly be killed? Do they know how it feels to be in the middle of a battle with artillery fire whizzing by, to be confronted by relentless and determined enemies, or to be scared so badly they can hardly breath, and unable to find a place of refuge? Can they tell you what they are really fighting for? They would undoubtedly say, "I am fighting for my country," without fully realizing what that really means. Are they too young to appreciate those defined and undefined freedoms that they have taken for granted without a lot of thought or understanding? However, I feel certain that by the time they touch down on American soil after their stints are over, they have a new perspective of freedom.

The young will never know what old men know: There are no permanent victors in war and that the vanquished survive and ultimately revive, stronger and better than before. The old already know the answer to the question "What have the victors gained? *What?*" The old would say, "Nothing. Nothing but a lot of heartache and misery."

"There is no glory in war—only good men dying terrible deaths." Hal Moore in "We Are Soldiers Still...."

Being young is a great gift that probably only a few young people appreciate. But there comes a time when we all, inevitably, will look back and wonder where the years have gone. I have been young, and I am growing old, and I pray that the young men and women of today will not be sent to fight battles that perhaps should not be fought, as I and a lot of my fellow soldiers were. I would do it again, so I make this statement in hindsight. I would hope, though, if the battle is worthy, the young will stand and fight to defend the freedoms and way of life they have enjoyed in the best place in the world, the Republic of the United States of America.

After my father's death, I found a letter in his scrapbook, which I wrote in Tokyo, Japan, a week before Christmas 1968, when I was feeling sad and depressed: "This death and killing, I want out. I'm just becoming human again, but for a while, that may be questionable. There is a young SOG Lieutenant in the hospital here, and today I gave him a tour of the grounds in his wheelchair. A brass band was playing 'God Rest Ye Merry Gentlemen' soft and doleful. I looked at the Lieutenant and wondered if he was tearing up the way I was and then I realized he had no eyes left. They had been blown away by mortar fire."

This memory, finally, is enough to push me over the edge. I began to cry for days on end. Intermittently, the tears stopped, but started again at the slightest provocation. The tears succeeded in washing away and drowning some of my memories. At long last, I was beginning to grieve and continue to fulfill my seemingly ordained destiny. A lot of my war buddies never had that opportunity, or maybe, I think, it was their destiny to die young.

Vietnam's fifth lesson finally seeped in. The dead, the wounded, the ill, are not guilty of what happened to them. I have learned to apply that to myself.

Never again has there been a conflict in my life between the Pfeifers of Park Avenue and the Churches of Death Valley Days. I have been both. I have been whatever I needed to be at any given moment to stay alive. In 1969 or 1970, if anyone had posed the question to me, "Do you think you will ever be normal again?" I might have answered, "I do not know. I do not know how normal feels or looks anymore. If how I feel now is normal, then no, I will never be normal again." If that same question were posed today, I would probably answer, "sometimes."

I am learning to be content. My journey that began so uncertain early on has become certain. Fraught with love, anger, hate, sorrow, fear, despair, and sometimes downright stupidity, it has returned to love.

**MOTHER, CHARLENE & FATHER, CHARLES
IN THE 70S**

CHUCK IS ABOUT TO SCORE

DAD & UNCLE AT MILLROSE GAMES

**WEST POINT FOOTBALL BEFORE
SURGERIES NULLIFIED MY CAREER**

"AM I GONNA MAKE IT" 1968

CHUTIN' UP 30/5/68

CHUCK AND THE SERGEANT MAJOR OF FOB 4

2nd BAT. 34TH INFANTRY COMMENDATION LETTER.

CHUCK & HIS MEN, HATCHET FORCE FOB-4

CHUCK & HIS MEN WITH COL. ARONS, 5TH SPECIAL FORCES GROUP

CAPT. CHUCK ON THE BEACH AT FOB-4

**RECON TEAM OF CHINESE
NUNGS WITH U.S. ADVISOR**

**NORTH VIETNAMESE COMMANDOS
WHO ATTACKED FOB-4 ON 8/23/1968**

**NUNGS' QUARTERS AFTER 8/23/1968,
NORTH VIETNAMESE ATTACK**

NO. VIETNAMESE BASKET CHARGES

NUNGS BARRACKS AFTER 8/23/68

NATIONAL WINSTON AD IN THE 70s

CHUCK & GEN. VO NGUYEN GIAP 1993

**OLIVER STONE & CHUCK ON SET OF
WALL STREET**

CHARLIE SHEEN & CHUCK IN WALL STREET

ANTHONY, JIMMY & CHUCK IN NIXON

EDDIE, CHUCK, ROBYN, IN BOOMERANG

WILLEM DAFOE, CHUCK & TOMMY SIZEMORE

**GRACE & CHRIS MEIGHER,
NORMAN MAILER & CHUCK**

CHRISTOPHER WALKEN & CHUCK

love from { Elaine Flanso 12/2/02

**THE QUEEN AND HER COURT
WORLD-FAMOUS ELAINE KAUFMAN
"ELAINE'S" RESTAURANT**

CHUCK'S ANNUAL CHRISTMAS LUNCH

CHUCK, WILLEM DAFOE, CHRISTOPHER WALKEN & GIADA COLAGRANDE

CHUCK ON HIS WAY TO MAPLECROFT FARM IN IPSWICH, MA. 1969

HARLEY BOY IN THE 80s

LOOKING FOR PHEASANT

CHUCK HUNTING IN SOUTH DAKOTA

THE GANG HUNTING QUAIL

LISA CROSBY PFEIFER 2016

CHUCK & LISA CHRISTMAS 2014

CHUCK'S AWARDS & ACCOMPLISMENTS

•

PHILANTHROPIST
HERO OF THE OPPRESSED

CASUAL HREO
WORLD TRAVELER

CAPT. CHARLES. F. PFEIFER

C & C DET. F.O.B. " 4

Soldier of Fortune Specializing in Civil Wars

FAREASTERN INDOCHINA SPECIAL FORCES
AND JUNGLE FIGHTER'S ASSOCIATION, LTD.

WARS FOUGHT
REVOLUTIONS STARTED
ASSASSINATIONS PLOTTED
GOVERNMENTS RUN
UPRISINGS QUELLED

TIGERS TAMED
BARS EMPTIED
VIRGINS CONVERTED
COMPUTERS VERIFIED
ORGIES ORGANIZED

GLOSSARY

Arc Light: B-52 Bomb Support Of Ground Troops
ARNV: Army of the Republic of North Vietnam
Baksheesh: Small Amount of Money
Beaucoup: Large Amount
BOQ: Bachelor Officers Quarters
Bright Light: Rescue Ops. W/Tact.Air Support
C-123: Small Cargo Plane. Caribou
C-130: Large Prop Carrier Plane
CAR-15: Carbine Version Of M16
CAS: Close Air Support
Charlie: Enemy Soldiers
CIDG: Civilian Irregular Defense Group
Cobra AH-1G: Attack Helicopter.
Danish Jaeger Forces: Elite SF Danish Army
Daiwi (Die we): Captain
Dead Bug: Falling Down Arms & Legs Up
Deuce-And-A-Half: 2-1/2 Ton Cargo Truck
Danish Jaeger Forces: Elite Special Forces
Deutsch Kampfschwimmer: German Frogmen
Du Ma, Doo-Mommie: Fuck Mother
EOC: Emergency Ops. Center
FOB: Forward Operational Base
French Marine Commandos: SF, like Navy SEAL
Hatchet Force: Special Operations Team
Hellenic Raiders: Greek 1st Raider/Paratroopers Gr.
Hooch Or Hootch: Improvised Living
Hot LZ: Landing Zone Under Fire

House 22: Safe House
I Corps: Tactical Military Quadrant
ICEVG: First Combat Evaluation Group
John Wayne: Expose to Danger
Kwah: Strong
Lay Chilly: Stop All Action
Marble Mountain: Five-Peak Mountain
MACV SOG: Military Assistance Command VN
      Special Ops. Group
Montagnard: Mixed Origin People. Yards
NVA: North Vietnam Army
Nung: Chinese Descent Ethnic Gr.
One Zero: Recon Team Leader
P: Piaster. About One Cent
PAVN: Peoples Army of Vietnam
Piss Tube: Makeshift Bathroom
PTSD: Post Traumatic Stress Disorder
Prairie Fire: Emergency Tactical Support
Project Eldest Son: Altered Weapons Program
RSVN: Republic of South Vietnam
SAS: Special Air Service
SF: Special Forces
Sapper: NVA Special Combatant
SOG: Studies & Observations Group
Sou: Coin. Small Amount
Special Forces Legionnaires: Fr. Foreign Legion
Spooky: Armed Transport Plane, C-130 or C-123
Tet: Major Attack By NVA And Viet Cong
     On South Vietnam, the U.S. and Allies

CPSIA information can be obtained
at www.ICGtesting.com
Printed in the USA
BVOW07*1253281117
501477BV00001B/1/P